MALTA STRIKES BACK

MAJOR-GENERAL R. E. URQUHART, C.B., D.S.O.
Commander of the Malta Brigade.

MALTA STRIKES BACK

THE STORY OF
231 INFANTRY BRIGADE
BY
MAJOR R. T. GILCHRIST
(INTELLIGENCE OFFICER 231 BDE. 1941-1943)

The Naval & Military Press Ltd

Published by

The Naval & Military Press Ltd
Unit 5 Riverside, Brambleside
Bellbrook Industrial Estate
Uckfield, East Sussex
TN22 1QQ England

Tel: +44 (0)1825 749494

www.naval-military-press.com
www.nmarchive.com

*In reprinting in facsimile from the original, any imperfections are inevitably reproduced
and the quality may fall short of modern type and cartographic standards.*

Foreword

BY

MAJOR-GENERAL R. E. URQUHART, C.B., D.S.O.

I CONSIDER MYSELF EXTREMELY FORTUNATE to have had the privilege of commanding the 231 Malta Brigade Group during a very active and exciting stage of its operational service overseas. When I took over the Brigade it was refitting in Egypt after its ordeal in Malta, where it had been subject to incessant air attack over a long period. All three battalions in the Brigade proper were Regular and many of the personnel had been abroad since before the war.

I was very impressed from the moment I saw them. At first the men were finely drawn and had obviously suffered, not only from the mental strain of the bombing but also from shortage of food. Their spirit, however, was undaunted and they set to in a most creditable way to learn everything they could during the intensive training period before the invasion of Sicily. We were given one of the most interesting tasks of any formation during the Sicily campaign. We were an independent Brigade Group and all ranks were intensely proud of the fact. We had our own Brigade sign and it was not long before the Maltese Cross was as well known as any of the other signs of the larger formations who had already had much battle fighting in North Africa.

The Brigade Group behaved magnificently and I am certain few formations could have carried out with quite the same degree of success and with the same courage many of the operations which it was called upon to perform. The excellence of their spirit and of the state of training within units was amply proved throughout Sicily and again when they carried out a left hook up the coast of Italy in the early days of the invasion of that country. In the latter operation events did not work out according to plan and it was this high standard of training and of the trust of all ranks which converted what might have been an unfortunate operation into a very marked success.

I was very sorry indeed when the time came for me to say good-bye to them. The Brigade Group had seen much fighting and had also been very successful.

Capt. Gilchrist, who has written this book, and Colonel Valentine, who has aided and abetted and supervised the preparation, were with the Brigade from its inception and went through with it the difficult times in Malta and later the operations in the Mediterranean. Both are well qualified to deal with the story in those days, and their interest in the regiments which they knew so well has enabled them to follow their progress until the conclusion of the fighting.

This is a story of which all those who had the privilege to play a part may well be proud.

R. E. Graham.
Maj. Gen.

ZONE ONE, B.L.A.
12th August, 1945.

Contents

		page
CHAPTER I.	THE MALTA BACKGROUND	1
II.	OUT OF THE FRYING-PAN	18
III.	THE LANDING	36
IV.	THE ROAD TO NOTO	44
V.	ON TO VIZZINI	48
VI.	VIZZINI	54
VII.	QUEEN OF THE HILLS	60
VIII.	THE CROSSING OF THE RIVER DITTAINO	65
IX.	SOUTH OF AGIRA	71
X.	CHANGE DIRECTION RIGHT	89
XI.	REGALBUTO RIDGE	96
XII.	MALTA—MARZAMEMI—MESSINA	106
XIII.	LEFT HOOK	113
XIV.	THE OLD ORDER CHANGES	131

Illustrations

The Brigade Sign of 231 Brigade	*Cover*
Major-General R. E. Urquhart, C.B.E., D.S.O.	*Frontispiece*
The continuous watch against invasion	*facing page* 4
Mobile Training without Petrol	8
Over the Walls	13
The versatile Army	16
The Navy does it again	43
Vizzini	55
Fighting Men	70
The view from the German O.P. at Agira	85
Regalbuto	108
Messina	113

Maps

The Plan of the Landing (Sicily)	38
The Crossing of the River Dittaino by 1 Hamps	67
231 Bde. positions South of Agira (19 July, 1943)	73
Company Positions of 1 Hamps (25 July, 1943)	82
Regalbuto and Regalbuto Ridge	98
The Plan of the Landing (Italy)	117
The Route of 231 Brigade	132

CHAPTER I

THE MALTA BACKGROUND

231 INFANTRY BRIGADE has also been known at various times since the outbreak of war as the Malta Infantry Brigade, the Southern Infantry Brigade, and the 1st (Malta) Infantry Brigade. It has at times contained as many as five battalions, and a detachment of tanks; and the 8th King's Own, the 2nd Bn. The Queen's Royal West Kent Regiment, the 2nd and 3rd Bns. King's Own Malta Regiment have all been under command of the Brigade for varying periods. It was in the early part of 1941 that the Brigade stabilized round a nucleus of three Regular battalions and began to acquire a personality of its own. These three battalions were 2nd Bn. The Devonshire Regiment, 1st Bn. The Hampshire Regiment and 1st Bn. The Dorsetshire Regiment. It was purely coincidental that the three counties from which these regiments were drawn should have adjoining boundaries in the South-West of England.

Life in the Brigade area at the end of the year 1941 was extremely comfortable, so much so that a casual visitor might well have obtained a wrong impression, particularly if he had come from England, which was just beginning to feel the rigours of rationing. He would have found a land of plenty, with almost unlimited quantities of food and drink, and a choice of about twelve places of entertainment. Parties and dances were given at clubs, and the sportsman had the choice of cricket, squash rackets, tennis, boating, hockey, and Rugby and Association football according to the season, and the finest bathing in the world. The troops were, for the most part, billeted in houses or public buildings such as schools, but where it was necessary for men to live in pillboxes everything was done to make them as homelike as possible. It was a common sight to see a vegetable garden and a chicken-run within the perimeter wire. Business and the social rounds were intermingled. Parties followed conferences, and it was not unusual for an officer to start out with the object of visiting four or five places and then find he was unable to complete his programme because of the overwhelming hospitality of the first two.

In those days there seemed little prospect of ever getting away from the Island as long as the war continued, and it was the policy laid down by Higher Authority that life should be made as comfortable as possible during what was obviously going to be a long siege. What the casual visitor would not have realized was that these men who were living such a carefree existence had already been proved by the heavy bombing which followed the entry of Italy into the war, and on the famous occasion of the stay of the aircraft carrier *Illustrious* in the Grand Harbour. The same visitor would have been astonished if he could have had a sight of the Malta Command Defence Scheme, which showed how thorough and complicated were the Island's defences down to the smallest detail. And not only was the defence catered for, but the Island had enormous aggressive power. From the hundreds of miles covered by the long-range bombers down to the distance of a bayonet thrust, Malta was armed to strike back and to strike hard at all enemies.

The role of the Southern Infantry Brigade was mainly defensive—only to become offensive in the case of an invasion. The Brigade area had thirty miles of coastline, twenty miles of which was suitable for sea landings. The Brigade area also contained a seaplane base, an aerodrome used by R.A.F. fighters and torpedo-carrying aircraft of the Fleet Air Arm, two emergency landing strips and a dispersal area for aircraft. Also in the Brigade area were vital installations of all kinds belonging to the Navy, the R.A.F. and the Ack-Ack and Coastal Artillery. The defensive tasks of the Brigade came under two main headings: firstly, defence from sea-borne invasion and, secondly, a defence from air-borne invasion. To counter the danger of sea-borne invasion, the Brigade manned concrete pillboxes sited in depth from the coast inland in three distinct lines. These posts were seldom more than 500 yards apart, and were designed to give covering and protecting fire to each other. The defence provided by the network of posts was supplemented by a continuous belt of wire along beaches, by numerous anti-tank and anti-personnel minefields, and by an anti-tank ditch. The fields in Malta are usually very small; each one is surrounded by a large stone wall, and there is a tendency for them to run in terraces. Because of this it was considered that air invasion was only possible on the levelled and open spaces of airfields, landing ground and dispersal areas. The defence of these open spaces was organized on exactly the same principle as on the coast, and the troops were placed in pillboxes around the perimeter of airfields. It will be seen that the defence of the Brigade was almost entirely static. The only mobility lay in the limited counter-attack role against aerodromes that was allotted to a few companies. Altogether, the Brigade manned over 150 posts. The fire-power of these posts was formidable. They were section posts and most of them contained a machine gun and an anti-tank rifle in addition to the Bren gun and usual section weapons.

This state of static defence continued until the end of 1941, but in December, 1941, two events occurred which were to make great changes in the life of everyone in the Brigade. On 10th of December the Luftwaffe returned to Sicily. On Christmas Eve the command of the Brigade was taken over by Brigadier K. P. Smith, O.B.E. Brigadier Smith had achieved great successes in the training of his battalion in England. He was not satisfied that the defence of the Brigade area, based entirely on pillboxes, would stand up to the new and improved technique of the Germans for attacking such fortified positions. Therefore he immediately commenced to reorganize the defences on a more mobile footing, without ignoring the advantages that such stout concrete emplacements would give to the defence.

On New Year's Eve there was a scare—a special D.R. was sent round with a message to all battalion commanders warning them that invasion was imminent. The momentous year 1942 had begun.

This action was explained in the following letter from Malta Command, dated 14th January, 1942:

"The following telegram has been received from C.-in-C., Mediterranean:

"'From chance remarks dropped by prisoners of war on board, it is indicated that a full-scale attack employing German troops on Malta may be contemplated in the immediate future.'

"This may well be a further example of the war of nerves: it will be forwarded down to Lt.-Cols. Comds. and sufficient copies are attached for this purpose.

"2. His Excellency has, however, decided, as a precautionary measure, that the state of preparedness of the Fortress will be increased to 'Asia Minor,' which except as stated in para. 3 below will come into effect forthwith.

"3. Minefields will NOT be laid at present."

January, 1942, was mainly notable for the advent of Major-General D. M. W. Beak, V.C., D.S.O., M.C., who took over the command of the Army in Malta.

Shortly after his arrival, General Beak gave a lecture to all officers in the Command. Few who attended that lecture will ever forget it. "You will do P.T. every morning before breakfast," said the General. "You will cycle in full equipment for twenty miles." "You will run and walk alternately for fifteen miles in full equipment." "You're lazy and some of you are too fat," he said, fixing his eye on one major renowned for his high standard of living.

It was not long before the Luftwaffe began to make its presence felt. At first the bombing was cautious. Three J.U.88's would come over, three or four times a day, escorted by a large number of fighters. After a time the confidence of the Germans rose, and raids increased to about eight a day, and often five J.U.88's were used in place of the familiar formation of three. The targets were airfields and dispersal areas and occasionally the dockyard. This was high-level bombing, and the tactics were extremely successful. It was a common sight to see as many as three Wellington bombers blazing on the ground in the vicinity of the Safi strip.

There was little that we could do about it. The bombing was done from such a height that only occasionally could the heavy A.A. score a direct hit. The light A.A. artillery was outranged. Our fighter aircraft (at that time Hurricanes without cannons) were outnumbered in the air by the M.E.109's. They were little faster than the J.U.88's and on the occasions when they were able to make an interception machine-gun fire proved insufficient to shoot down the bombers, unless a lucky hit penetrated the heavy armour of the J.U.88.

In January the first calls were made on the Brigade to provide working parties for construction work on aerodromes. The Brigade was constantly to find working parties for the rest of the year. At first demands were modest, but after a time every man in the Brigade who was not required in a vital operational role, after the maximum thinning out of defences, was employed on some kind of labouring work.

During this month the Brigade held several exercises designed to test communications, and to try out the new defensive plan based on the employment of a much greater mobile reserve.

During this month also a system of Infantry O.Ps. was established all over the Island. This Brigade manned three O.Ps. The function of an O.P. was to give immediate information to Brigade Headquarters in case of an air-borne landing. Their efficiency in this respect was never tested, but they were to do useful work in spotting crashed aircraft and our own and enemy pilots who had baled out. They kept a record of all bombing,

[Crown Copyright Reserved
THE CONTINUOUS WATCH AGAINST INVASION.
The O.P. of the 1st Hampshire Regiment on Sheleile Tower, Malta.

and useful statistics were compiled by Brigade and Malta Command as a result of their observations.

The year 1942, as far as Malta was concerned, was divided up into two periods. There was the period of bombing and the period of famine. Throughout the month of February the bombing continued on the same scale as in the last days of January. Only strictly military targets were attacked, and anyone not in the vicinity of these targets was reasonably safe. The unfortunate men who were on working parties in the centre of airfields were in a poor position, and casualties were sustained. During the night the enemy adopted "intruder" tactics with a succession of single bombers continually over the Island. For the ordinary individual these raids were more dangerous than the bigger daylight raids, as bombs were scattered indiscriminately throughout the Island, especially when the aircraft were caught in an A.A. barrage or searchlight concentration.

The result of this bombing began to have its effect on the life of the troops. Owing to their proximity to the Grand Harbour and submarine base, Valetta and Sliema were beginning to take a greater proportion of the bombing, and it was no longer advisable to visit these places on leave. Two cinemas had received direct hits, and in one of these—the Regent Cinema, Valetta—there were heavy casualties among civilians and Army personnel.

During the month of March the enemy changed his bombing tactics completely. By this time he had knocked out nearly all our bombers on the ground, and the fighter effort that the R.A.F. were able to make was puny compared with the number of enemy fighters in the sky. Therefore, instead of using J.U.88's in small formations the enemy concentrated on mass attacks. From two to five attacks were made during the daylight hours, in which anything from thirty to seventy bombers with strong fighter cover took part. During a mass attack, which lasted on an average for twenty minutes, the bombers approached in waves, each wave containing from five to about thirty bombers. Usually J.U.88's were seen, but J.U.87's were also used in these attacks. The latter had not been seen over the Island since the early part of 1941.

The first target for these heavy bombing raids was Ta Kali aerodrome, and for several days the aerodrome was rendered unserviceable, much damage being done to aircraft on the ground, buildings and installations. This was followed by heavy raids on Luqa and Hal Far aerodromes and on the Safi strips and adjoining dispersal areas.

No convoys had reached Malta with supplies since November, 1941. On 23rd March three ships reached Malta out of an original convoy of four ships. This was a wonderful triumph for the Royal Navy, as the convoy had been bombed the whole way from Alexandria. From the moment of their arrival in Malta these ships came under heavy dive-bombing. Two of the ships reached the Grand Harbour, but were sunk before much of the cargo had been discharged. The third ship, H.M.S. *Breconshire*, was slightly damaged, and had to be anchored off Zonkor Point in rough seas, and was eventually towed round to Marsa Sirocco Bay, where it was attacked several times by Stukas and eventually sunk by a bomb from a J.U.88.

Spitfires began to make a welcome appearance in the air, but they were hopelessly outnumbered by the enemy fighters. Perhaps the most heroic sight throughout a heroic year was to see about half a dozen of these fighters in the air taking on all comers. They were frequently shot down, but seldom without first having scored a success against their opponents.

Although the enemy had great success and caused a great deal of damage to property and installations on the ground, they had accomplished little of their avowed task to neutralize Malta. This was entirely due to the gallant work of the R.A.F., and the equally gallant manner in which the gunners continually manned and fired the heavy and light A.A. guns. Casualties in the Brigade this month were on the increase, but they were still remarkably light. Six men had been killed and thirteen injured, but only two of these injuries were of a serious nature. Damage to Army property and equipment was negligible. Although the enemy still concentrated on military targets, there were no longer safe places in the Island. The Headquarters of Malta Command at Lascaris Barracks received a direct hit, and Colonel Clinch, the G.S.O.1, was killed.

Throughout April the bombing continued with the same intensity. The following extract from the War Diary of the 2nd Devons illustrates the sort of things that happened in a single raid:

" 0947 hrs. Air-raid warning. A large number of J.U.87's and J.U.88's attacked Kalafrana and Ta Silch areas. No. 5626532 U./L./Cpl. Leonard Percy Galton, ' A ' Coy., was killed at Dowdalls Hotel (W/T Cadre) and the following were slightly injured: L./Cpl. Barnes (Carrier Pln.), L./Cpl. May (' A ' Coy.) and Cpl. Sear (' E ' Coy.). The buildings and hangars at Kalafrana suffered severe damage and a small fire was caused in the Gzira Petrol Station. Post R.33 received a hit and corner of post was knocked off. There were no casualties in this post. Bombs were also dropped on the Hal Far aerodrome and in Weid Znuber area. The All Clear was sounded at 1255 hrs."

The reference to Post R.33 is interesting. This post, which was situated near the station buildings of Hal Far aerodrome, had received over forty bombs within the perimeter wire. Even when at last it sustained a direct hit, no damage was caused to the occupants, which illustrates the stoutness of the material with which these posts were constructed.

At the end of this month the bombing reached its height of intensity. The daily number of bombers which were over Malta for one week was:

	J.U. 88	J.U. 87	TOTAL
19th April	120	71	191
20th April	235	62	297
21st April	100	40	140
22nd April	136	43	179
23rd April	106	30	136
24th April	124	33	157
25th April	220	39	259
			1,359

N.B.—These figures do not include night raiders or escorting and patrolling fighters.

Here are the figures of bomb tonnages dropped on various places in Malta during the month of April. The total tonnage is greater than any monthly tonnage of bombs dropped on the United Kingdom at the height of the blitz:

Ta Kali	...	841 tons
Hal Far	...	750½ „
Luqa	...	804½ „
Kalafrana	...	196 „
Dockyard	...	3,156½ „
Elsewhere	...	980 „
Total	...	6,728½ „

Hal Far and Kalafrana were in the Brigade area, and the Brigade received a large percentage of bombs aimed at Luqa and the Dockyard area as well as the bombs alleged to have been dropped elsewhere. To say that over 2,000 tons of bombs were dropped in the Brigade area over this period would be a fair claim.

The men stood up to this bombing well, and the civilians responded to their example magnificently.

On 21st April Major-General Beak delivered the following special message:

" I wish you all to know how much I appraise and appreciate the steadfast and excellent work you have been giving and still are to our cause which is the cause of all free peoples.

" You have been experiencing a tense period fraught with intense difficulties. Nevertheless, you have responded gallantly and never once failed or faltered. You are sticking to the job with a cheerfulness and fortitude which is beyond praise. Much has been asked of you, but more have you given.

" I know you are straining at the leash to be able to get at the enemy. Nothing can be more trying than having to ' sit and take it.' The day will come when we shall ' rise and give it ' and then I know that you will not be ' weighed in the balance and found wanting.'

" There must be many questions passing through your minds which cannot, at the moment, be answered. Remember that there are no points in the present situation which are forgotten and no efforts lacking to see it through to a successful conclusion.

" Your spirited work is known and praised the world over, but nowhere is it better known, more understood and appreciated, than in this Island by those of us who are fully in the picture.

" Your effort is magnificent. You may be justly proud."

One result of the bombing was that working parties were asked to do a different type of work, and for the next two months the Brigade rendered great assistance to the Civil Government in clearing the debris, especially at Ghain Dueili Tunnel and the Marsa Basin area. Another task was the retrieving of large quantities of R.A.S.C. stores which were buried under the ruins of buildings.

It was during this month that the Dorsets and Devons each did a two-day mobile exercise with the full battalion. It was extremely difficult to take away a complete battalion from its operational commitments and at the same time to ensure complete freedom from working parties for two days. Nevertheless, the effort had to be made, because owing to the continuous working parties no Brigade exercises had been possible since January.

Both exercises were based on the same plan, first a march of about ten miles to a concentration area, brushing light enemy opposition away *en route*, then a night in bivouac, and finally

MOBILE TRAINING WITHOUT PETROL.
2nd Bn. The Devonshire Regiment, Malta.

[Crown Copyright Reserved

in the morning a forced march followed by a full-scale attack. Because of the limits enforced by the size of the Island, the route of the exercise was almost a complete circle, with the final attack being put in not far from the starting point. This route was chosen to avoid as much as possible casualties through enemy bombing. They were curious exercises because they took place on two of the heaviest days of bombing that Malta has ever experienced. There was nothing " exercise " about the danger from the air, and passing the much-bombed Marsa Basin was like running a gauntlet. On the day the Dorsets held their exercise, the Germans made their first deliberate raid on the city of Valetta.

By this time the Bofors (light A.A.) were running out of ammunition, and this must have been obvious to the Germans, for the Messerschmitt fighters began to dive low and shoot up men on the ground. To counteract this, battalions were permitted to fire small arms at low-flying aircraft, and additional machine guns were mounted along the airfields and landing strips. A Messerschmitt 109 was shot down immediately, and was credited jointly to the Devons and Dorsets. Within a fortnight two more had been shot down. These were the only aircraft which could be positively claimed, but many bombers and fighters were riddled with bullets fired by the Infantry, and the Germans, quick to realize and correct their mistakes, gave up their low-flying exploits.

April was Malta's worst month of bombing. Every possible type of projectile was hurled from the sky—mines, 4,000-lb. " Satan " bombs, armour-piercing rocket bombs, assortments of H.E. from 100 to 2,000 lbs., and thousands of small anti-personnel bombs.

Casualties in the Brigade for the month were one officer and fourteen other ranks killed, and two officers and fourteen other ranks wounded. The reason for the small number of casualties lay in the fact that by now all troops had become expert at dispersal and taking cover. Nevertheless, for the first time the Germans had gained the initiative to such an extent that they were beginning to regulate the tempo of our lives. Work could only be done between long periods spent in slit trenches or shelters, and a battalion exercise of the Hamps had to be cancelled because it exposed the troops to too much danger from the air.

For the first few days of May the enemy bombing continued with the same intensity. The position was now becoming very serious. The Dockyard and submarine base had been put out of action. The Germans had complete mastery in the air, and from the end of April they had begun to select A.A. gun sites and Army barracks and camps as their targets. These were clearly pre-invasion tactics. The enemy had removed the striking-power of the Navy and bombing aircraft, and fighter protection of the Island was practically nil. Only the A.A. defence stood in the way of invasion, and with ammunition running low it appeared as if this would be neutralized within a month. Something had to be done quickly. The first effort was to fly in fifty Spitfires from an aircraft carrier, but most of these were knocked out on the ground before they could materially affect the position. Then came the famous victory of 10th May. On 9th May, unknown to the enemy, the Island received a large reinforcement of Spitfires. On 10th May H.M.S. *Welshman*, a minelaying cruiser, brought the badly needed supplies of Bofors ammunition. This ship was unloaded by the Infantry in record time, and the ammunition dispatched straight to the gun positions. The early morning reconnaissance planes on the 10th must have disclosed to the Germans that there was a cruiser in the harbour. The Germans came in their usual confident way with waves of J.U.88's and Stukas, but they were surprised to find over sixty Spitfires in the air waiting for them, and also to be met by the heaviest A.A. barrage that had been seen for months. Despite the danger, practically everyone—both soldiers and civilians alike—stood in the open to watch the battle. As the enemy bombers dived through the intense concentration and barrage so our fighters went in after them. Planes were dropping out of the sky, in bits and pieces, from all angles. In that raid alone the enemy lost 63 aircraft, either destroyed or so badly damaged that they were unlikely to regain their base.

It had taken the Germans three months to gain superiority in the air over Malta. Now the British had regained it in one raid. Although the Germans tried very hard for another week to regain the advantage, they were quite unsuccessful, and they lost over 200 aircraft in the attempt. That was the end of the mass bombing raids on Malta, with one exception much later in the year. The Germans resorted to small nuisance raids, usually carried out from a high level, and when these proved costly they even bullied the wretched Italians into making an appearance over the Island.

That the enemy was contemplating a landing assault was clearly shown by the increase of enemy E-boat activity around the Island, and especially off the strip of coastline guarded by the Brigade. An Italian came ashore and was captured in the

Dorsets' sector, and from information given by this prisoner it appeared that the enemy were testing our coastal defences with a view to making a raid.

The Brigade War Diary records: " During the month nearly all the troops in this Brigade who are not manning key positions have been engaged in construction work on aerodromes, and salvage work clearing up the damage caused by the heavy bombing in the previous month. The work on aerodromes has consisted of building pens to protect aircraft, and standing by to fill in craters and thus keep the aerodromes serviceable. As a result of these working parties anything in the nature of an uninterrupted training programme has been impossible."

It is difficult to state exactly what feelings lurked in the minds of the men about this time. Certainly they were not aware of how serious the situation had really been. To them life must have been an endless drudgery with periods of great danger. The danger they stood up to with great bravery. Not a single instance of shirking or cowardice was reported, but heroism was always present when opportunities arose. Several cases were reported of the rescue of civilians from damaged houses when unexploded bombs were in the vicinity and H.E. bombs were raining all round. Fires in aircraft were extinguished, and pilots dragged clear, although the bombs or torpedoes on these craft might have exploded at any minute. These chances, however, fell to a few men only, but all had the difficult job of " sitting and taking it." The awards that were granted to officers and men of the Hampshire company who defended the Safi strip and the Devon company that defended Hal Far were well deserved.

Perhaps the hardest thing of all to bear was the feeling in the mind of everyone, that existence on Malta was like a life sentence in prison without hope of reprieve. The resistance which most of us had to put up was not so much against the danger of bombing but against a most morbid depression. In the case of many of the men this feeling was counteracted by the fiction of " the boat." However improbable it seemed to those in the know, these men always expected a boat to arrive to take them home. The more realistic did not have this consolation, and it was imperative that something would have to be done about it immediately.

By this time, every place of entertainment in Malta had been knocked out by the bombing. There were no rest camps to go to; it was quite useless to take leave because of the lack of accommodation and the difficulty over rations in a food shortage which was just beginning to make itself felt. The lighting supply had failed throughout the Island, and the water supply was very erratic. Beer was no longer brewed in Malta, and the N.A.A.F.I. was able to do little to supplement rations. There was a shortage of everything: food, drink, paper, petrol, oil for lighting and cooking; and the shortage appeared likely to increase until these commodities disappeared entirely.

Up to this time the Brigade had been little different from any other brigade in Malta, but now a new virility was to appear, which was to raise the Brigade above the normal and bring it triumphantly through the hardest times of all which lay ahead.

Throughout June and July the food shortage increased, and when at the end of July the Eighth Army had fallen back to the line at Alamein, and only two ships had reached Malta out of several convoys which had made the attempt, it might be imagined that we had reached a stage when we were prepared to throw our hands in. But such was far from being the case.

At this period in its history the Brigade had acquired a staff of key personnel who were to lead it successfully and unchanged for the next twelve months.

BRIGADE STAFF

Brigadier K. P. Smith, O.B.E.: Brigade Commander.
Major W. E. F. Tuffill: Brigade Major.
Capt. F. G. Sadleir: Staff Captain.
Capt. R. T. Gilchrist: Brigade I.O.
Capt. J. W. Jennings: Brigade T.O.
Capt. A. G. McTavish: Brigade S.O.

2ND BN. THE DEVONSHIRE REGIMENT

Lieut.-Colonel A. W. Valentine, M.B.E.: Commanding Officer.
Major G. R. Young: Second-in-Command.
Capt. I. F. H. Edgar: Adjutant.

1ST BN. THE HAMPSHIRE REGIMENT

Lieut.-Colonel J. L. Spencer, M.C.: Commanding Officer.
Major H. D. Nelson Smith: Second-in-Command.
Capt. I. Methven, M.B.E.: Adjutant.

1ST BN. THE DORSETSHIRE REGIMENT

Lieut.-Colonel W. H. B. Ray: Commanding Officer.
Major R. M. Nicol: Second-in-Command.
Capt. N. H. Golding: Adjutant.

OVER THE WALLS.
Men of the 2nd Bn. The Dorsetshire Regiment training in Malta.

[Crown Copyright Reserved

Brigadier Smith's contribution to the renaissance was his determination that all work should be of the highest standard, whatever the conditions.

Thus, despite the growing lack of food and the first signs of under-nourishment among the men, all labouring work, whether unloading convoys, building pens on aerodromes, or removing debris, had to be done at record speed. When on the rare occasions there was no labouring work to be done, the troops were immediately put on intensive training, a feature of which was the leaping over stone walls, which abound in Malta. Turn-out always had to be immaculate, so that we began to acquire a reputation for smartness not only in Malta but throughout the Middle East.

To maintain morale a large project of entertainment and sport was started in the Brigade area. This was the conception of the Brigade I.O. The difficulties in this organization were immense. For example: a promoter of a football league was faced with the problem that there were no footballs, no football boots, no football grounds and no transport to convey the teams about had the grounds existed. All these problems had somehow to be overcome or circumvented. The league, when it eventually started, was called the Spartan League, because everyone had to have a Spartan outlook to attempt to play under such difficulties. In the same way, before opening a cinema in the Brigade area a suitable hall had somehow to be acquired in an area where every inch of available house space was requisitioned. Electric light had to be produced on an island which had no lights; apparatus had to be constructed from bits and pieces found all over the Island; films had to be hired and the whole enterprise run at the promoter's risk, because there was no official Army backing for these schemes.

This entertainment project was only designed to last three months until conditions in the Island improved, but conditions improved so slowly that it lasted for nine months. During that time two cinemas and a theatre were opened in the Brigade area, and all troops in the vicinity benefited by these as well as Brigade troops. During this period of nine months over 500 cinema performances were given and thirty-three theatrical performances. These houses of entertainment had to support themselves and prices were cut to a minimum. Compared with current Malta prices of entertainment, this resulted in a saving of over £4,000 to the pockets of the troops. There was no assistance given by Command in the organizing and running of these cinemas. It was the voluntary work of a few individuals in which the lead was taken by the Brigade I.O., Capt. Chilton and C.S.M. Hill, of the Dorsets, and Lieut. Simpson, of Malta Tanks. In producing concert parties and revues the Brigade I.O. had the assistance of the battalions' dance bands and concert parties. The Devons particularly distinguished themselves with the quality of the shows which they put on at " Garrison Theatre."

This was a period of hard work and of hard play, and not only did the lead come from Brigade Staff. The battalions themselves branched out on their own account in this revival business. If there was a record to be had, the Hampshire Regiment set themselves to collect it. At a time when the weekly petrol allotment to a whole battalion was only 30 gallons, the Hampshires used only nine and a half gallons in a petrol-saving competition. Later they were to establish records for discharging cargoes. The Hampshires also contrived to run numerous tactical exercises, and it took all the ingenuity and humour of Lieut.-Colonel Spencer to make these exercises realistic in the difficult Malta conditions.

The Devons concentrated on a different type of exercise. Because of their location they were more closely connected with the Air Force, Fleet Air Arm and the Navy. Their exercises concerned the defence of Hal Far aerodrome and Kalafrana seaplane base. The Devons had always been the most nautical of the battalions, and during the summer months they ran swimming contests and boating regattas. They were the first battalion in Malta to experiment in the training for combined operations.

The Dorsets also were aquatic, but their strength lay in the organization of toughening and endurance exercises which they carried out with considerable ingenuity. They constructed the toughest form of obstacle course, combined with " battle inoculation," with exploding bombs, and live ammunition fired for a near miss.

By August the food shortage was becoming acute. There were some people who were not much affected, who never seemed unduly hungry or appeared to lose weight, but for most of us the months from June to December, 1942, were months of slow famine. Even after meals one still felt hungry. Many people lost weight at an alarming rate, and as much as 2 stones in weight was lost during the first few months. A soldier on active service is supposed to consume about 4,000 calories a day. The Malta ration scale consisted of 2,000 calories. The main catering problem was to produce a third meal in the day, and all sorts of ingenious tricks were resorted to so that something could be shown on the breakfast plate. The food shortage preyed constantly on the minds of most of us. The men could quote the lengthy ration scale backwards, and the duty officer going the rounds at meal times had an almost mathematical task to see that everyone had his fair share. Courts-martial about this period dealt mainly with cases of food theft. It was safer to leave a five-pound note lying about than a packet of biscuits. In officers' messes the situation was no better, and minute portions of butter, sugar and jam had to be put in separate dishes to make sure that the shares were equal, and to avoid unpleasant feelings and jealousies. Most people hated themselves for feelings which they never thought they possessed, but with hunger always present the stomach dictated to the mind.

It was impossible to supplement the Army rations with food purchased from outside sources, unless the purchaser was prepared to pay the black market prices. These prices varied considerably, and it was much easier to purchase by barter than by money, which was beginning to lose its value. The top prices ever quoted on the black market were as follows: one egg, 2s. 6d.; a cabbage, 3s.; a cauliflower, 2s. 6d.; a horse (for food), £60; sugar, 4s. per lb. The top price for flour caused statisticians to estimate that each loaf cost 10s. Imbid, the local wine—known to the troops as " Stuka juice "—rose from 6d. to 4s. 6d. per quart. Whisky and gin cost £4 and £3 per bottle respectively. It was quite impossible for the troops to purchase on the black market except to supplement their cigarette ration, and often they had to pay as much as 2s. 6d. for ten " V's " or Woodbines, or 3s. for ten cigarettes of the Player's, Gold Flake and Capstan categories.

It has already been stated that in June only two ships out of a much larger convoy arrived in Malta. A complicated organization had been worked out so that these ships could be discharged before the enemy had a chance of sinking them by bombing. The whole organization is admirably summed up in the General Staff Weekly Intelligence Summary for the week ended 20th June, 1942, of which the following is the relevant extract:

" A large number of ships were expected and, bearing in mind what happened to the last convoy to reach Malta, an intricate organization was built up in order that the ships should be unloaded and the cargoes dispersed in the shortest possible time. This required careful planning, as, due to the heavy attacks on the harbour during April, a large number of quays and docks were unserviceable and much preliminary clearance was necessary. Briefly, the organization was as follows:

" The actual unloading of the ships was carried out partly

by Naval and Army personnel and partly by Maltese stevedores: some of the winchmen and other skilled labour being provided by Army Docks Group personnel who came with the ships. Stores were unloaded direct to the quay or into the lighters. The unloading was the responsibility of the Navy as far as the quays or lighter points and from then on the Army took over the responsibility for getting the stores dispersed to dumps or consignees, if near at hand. The Army had therefore to provide in the Dockyard parties for unloading ships, parties for lighters, fire-fighting and dockside labour, tally clerks, messengers and telephonists, first-aid posts, a Docks Directorate, which was the central H.Q., and a party to operate the smoke screen over the harbour. To remove stores to dumps some 240 vehicles were provided, based on M.T. sub-depots, each of which had its own repair organization. Dumps, where all stores for distant consignees were to be dumped temporarily, were selected in sites where dispersal was compatible with a quick turn-round of M.T. so that a continual flow of M.T. to and from the various quays and lighter points could be maintained. Over all this was imposed a combined civil and military traffic organization to ensure the smooth flow of vehicles and civilian and military gangs for road clearance in the event of heavy bombing. The whole unloading was made a combined effort of first priority by the Navy, Army and Civil authorities, whilst the A.A. Artillery and R.A.F. provided the necessary protection. As work had to be carried out day and night it was necessary to work in shifts, and this meant that a total of 2,300 men daily on unloading the convoy, 1,700 on aerodromes and 350 vehicles were required which were supplied from the Army. This imposed considerable strain on man-power for defence requirements which were necessarily slightly intensified at the time and meant the stopping of leave.

"Although, as it is known, only two merchant ships, the *Orari* and *Troilus,* finally arrived, the organization was well tested and carried out the unloading of these two ships in record time. The ' bogy ' figure was 1,000 tons per day per ship. Tobruk had achieved 600 tons and we intended to beat it. Actually the figures for the two ships were:

    First 24 hours: 3,200 tons.
    First 48 hours: 8,000 tons.
    First 72 hours: 11,300 tons.
    First 108 hours: 15,000 tons.

[Crown Copyright Reserved

THE VERSATILE ARMY.

Men of the Malta Brigade working as Dock Labourers in the bomb-damaged Dockyard, Malta.

" In four and a half days, which was the period for which the Army worked, 15,000 tons, approximately, were unloaded and cleared from the quays. All the experts assure us that this is a most remarkable effort."

The June convoy did nothing to relieve the food shortage in Malta. It only prolonged our lives a little longer. By August those who knew the real situation realized that Malta could only withstand the siege a few weeks longer. Prodigious efforts were made by the Navy and Merchant Navy to get the supply ships through, and in one of the most heroic voyages in sea history they succeeded in getting through to Malta, battered but afloat, a convoy consisting of a tanker and four merchant ships. One of these, the *Melbourne Star*, was unloaded by the Brigade. By this time the air cover for convoys had increased out of all recognition and, apart from discharging cargoes, the Brigade now took on the task of maintaining aerodromes. A variety of tasks were undertaken, such as crater filling by day and by night, servicing aircraft by day, speedy removal of crashed aircraft by carriers, and the loading up of aircraft guns.

The nuisance raids by German and Italian aircraft by day and by night continued, but they diminished at the end of the year. Only once did the Germans try out their tactics of mass raids. This was in October, and they suffered as decisive a defeat as in May. They did not try again.

Whenever there was a lull in working parties the Brigade were quick to try out new methods of training. A combined operations exercise, comprising the capture of St. Lucian Fort, was worked out by the 2nd Devons, and all the battalions did this exercise in turn. Considering the limited amount of equipment available, the realism of this exercise was remarkable. Commando training was also carried out by selected companies and platoons.

With the success of the First and Eighth Armies in November, and the capture of Benghazi, the siege of Malta was raised. From now onwards until the end of the year a succession of small convoys sailed into the Grand Harbour, and all the great machinery for dealing with convoys was put into motion. Thus, until the end of the year every single man in the Brigade who could be spared from a vital operational role was employed as a stevedore in the docks or as a labourer on the aerodromes. The troops by this time had become expert at all forms of labouring work and especially at unloading ships. The Hampshires took most of the records, and perhaps their best achievement was the unloading of the s.s. *Robin Locksley* carrying 7,785 tons of cargo. Work was commenced on this ship at dawn on 20th November and the cargo was discharged and the ship cleared by 1800 hrs. on the 25th. Only on Christmas Day was the work suspended, when for the first time the men were given a full-size dinner. This proved too much for digestions that had known famine scale for six months, and many of them "just couldn't take it."

And so 1942, Malta's great year, drew to a close. As General Beak had stated: the role of the Infantry in Malta was the most difficult of all. They had " to sit and take it." They went through the ordeal of fire and famine, and they were tempered by it and won through to a new confidence and spirit of resolution. The 1st (Malta) Infantry Brigade had proved that they could " take it " and had also proved that they were worthy to be selected to strike back.

CHAPTER II

OUT OF THE FRYING-PAN

Our play is done, the story told:
Now sunset robs the bastions of their gold.
Let night bring down the curtain—but, oh, so silently,
For three grey ships in convoy are stealing out to sea.

IF you had lived on a small island for four and a half years, three and a half years, or two years, which had been the fate of the men of the three British battalions of the 1st (Malta) Infantry Brigade, and had shared the same times of perils and tribulations, it is natural that you should expect to find a close bond of friendship between the troops and the local inhabitants. The full extent of this friendship was not realized until 30th March, 1943, the day on which the Brigade left the Island. It had often been a subject for discussion how one day the Brigade were going to get off the Island, because our commitments were so great and our roots so deep. It had been argued that it would take months, but when the time really came it took exactly four days. It was a case of " up stick " and leave those remaining behind to sort out the mess.

During their stay on the Island many of the men had married Maltese wives, some had Maltese sweethearts, and all had made friends. It must have been a great shock to these people to know that their husbands and lovers were to be snatched away from them so suddenly. At first it appeared as if they were too stunned by the shock to make any emotional response, but when the day of parting came the real feelings of the Maltese for the British troops were revealed—full and unashamed. There was scarcely a dry eye that morning in the village of Tarxien when the column moved out for the last time. An even more amazing sight awaited the soldiers when they arrived at the Grand Harbour to embark on the transports. The magnificent bastions which tower upwards from the water of the harbour to the Citadel of Valetta were lined with people—each one waving a handkerchief in farewell. This waving of handkerchiefs from shore to ship and from ship to shore in reply continued all day, for the convoy did not sail until evening. Some wives and sweethearts who had already endured the punishment of one leave-taking hired dyghsa (the Maltese equivalent of a dinghy) and sailed round the ships in a second self-inflicted torture of parting. Eventually dusk fell, and as the long day ended the three grey ships sailed slowly out to sea taking the men of Hampshire, the men of Dorsetshire and the men of Devonshire with them. All eyes were turned to the Valetta side of the harbour, where the regimental band of the Royal West Kent Regiment played the regimental marches as each ship passed in turn. No one turned to look at the other side of the harbour, where on the headlands of St. Angelo and Senglea, L'Isle Adam, La Vallette and all the other knights of the first siege of Malta stood in ghostly array. All ears were too intent on the music to hear their farewell words—" Well done, well done. You also held the Island as an outpost of Christianity against the overwhelming forces of barbarism and evil."

The journey from Malta to Alexandria took four days and was without incident, which would not have been possible at any time during the previous two years. It demonstrated clearly the control that the Allies had obtained over the Mediterranean in the past four months. Perhaps a part of the credit for the safety of the journey may be claimed by the Brigade. Units had been asked before they sailed to stress the importance of suppressing idle talk concerning the move, and strict censorship of letters was imposed. Shortly after arrival in Egypt a letter was received from Lord Gort, V.C., the Governor of Malta, in which the Brigade was congratulated on the way in which it had cooperated in these measures, and which stated that not a single breach of security had been reported.

The ship berthed at Alexandria at approximately 5 p.m. on

3rd April, and the Brigade was welcomed to Egypt by Brigadier Smith, who had left Malta previously by air. Then the Brigade moved to 216 Transit Camp at Sidi Bishr. Night was falling as we reached the camp and everyone was feeling very tired. It had been one of those typically Army days. The forenoon had been spent in preparation for disembarkation with the usual succession of orders and counter-orders. The ships crept into the harbour at a snail's pace and then took a very long time to tie up alongside. Disembarkation had proceeded very slowly, and had been followed by an exceedingly uncomfortable journey for several miles in trucks. Looking back through the day it was impossible to say that any special physical or mental effort had been made, yet at the end most people felt exhausted and slightly bad-tempered. To make matters worse, insufficient accommodation had been provided at the camp, and it was not until the early hours of the morning that most people settled in for the night. Quartermasters had a particularly bad night.

Sandstorms, " big eats," entertainments and thieving Egyptians—those are the memories which most men of the Brigade will have of Sidi Bishr. It was unfortunate that during this period of rest we should hit the Egyptian equivalent of Buchan's cold spell, for the driving sand and cold winds made it uncomfortable for a brigade which was receiving its first experience of camping after years of Malta billets. After the bad start, the authorities did everything possible to make us happy. It was announced that our stay at Sidi Bishr would be devoted to rest and recreation. Entertainments by local organizations were provided on a large scale. An average of seven hundred men a day were entertained to free meals at clubs, theatrical shows or dances. A good time was had by all except a few unfortunate officers' who were responsible for the reorganization and re-equipping of the Brigade, which had left Malta almost in the nude as far as warlike stores were concerned.

In Malta anything above the normal in the way of food was always referred to by the men as " big eats." The ration scale was now increased to such an extent that digestive organs accustomed to " famine " scale were hard put to it to face the new situation. This supply of " big eats " produced two schools of thought and argument among the men : " Fattening us up so we won't look bad when we get home," said some. " Fattening us up for the kill, more like. We're on a stunt, you'll see," said others.

It is impossible not to admire a person who is expert at his own particular business or profession, and the Egyptian tent and rifle thieves were certainly masters of theirs. We were warned about them in advance, and guards and picquets were provided to meet the situation, but even so rifles and tents disappeared almost nightly. Their best effort was the removal of the complete sides of the very large tent that comprised the Officers' Mess of Brigade Headquarters. Towards the end of the stay at Sidi Bishr orders were given to shoot at any suspicious movement in the night, and it became extremely risky to move about the camp in darkness. For a few this was their first shot in anger.

For the move from Sidi Bishr to Mena Camp by rail the Brigade split up into two parties. For the first party the journey in cattle trucks across the flat fertile delta, and the stop halfway to " brew up " tea from water from the boiler of the engine proved delightful. If you really want to see a country I can recommend that you see it from a slow-moving cattle truck in glorious sunshine with your legs dangling over the side. But look out for point levers or you will be sent spinning overboard. The second party were unfortunate. They suffered all the usual Army delays and arrived in the new camp at about 3 o'clock in the morning.

Sidi Bishr had been half desert. I think it can be claimed that Mena Camp was in real desert, even though the fertility of the Nile Delta started in a sharply defined line only two miles away. The camp was within walking distance of the Sphinx and Great Pyramids, and many took the opportunity to visit and study these ancient monuments of Egyptian civilization—at any rate, many officers made that their excuse for a visit to the excellent bar of the Mena House Hotel under the shadow of the Pyramids.

The stay at Mena Camp was notable for two things. The first was the " dryshod " training. Now " dryshod " training means training for a combined naval and military sea landing on the dry land. Sitting in the sand, imagining that you are in a boat on the ocean can be very dull unless the training is carried out with experts who possess imagination. Lieut.-Colonel Stephenson and his training team certainly did their best for us. It was part of the training that all ranks should repeat aloud the role that they were going to play in the landing on foreign soil. " I am the platoon commander. I am the first man to leave the boat," said the officer. " I am the first man to be killed," the cynics would add. It was beginning to dawn on us how dangerous this combined operation might prove in reality. Nevertheless, despite this very specialized training, there were still many among the men who were convinced that we were going home.

It had become known while we were at Sidi Bishr that the Brigade was going to be converted into a Brigade Group, and it was during this period of training at Mena that the commanding officers of units who were to come under command reported for instructions. On 26th April Lieutenant-General Sir Oliver Leese, the Commander of XXX Corps, visited the Brigade and announced that the Brigade had now come under his command and consequently formed part of the Eighth Army. At the end of the month the Brigade Commander and a few selected members of the Brigade Staff were let into the secret of what it was all about. On arrival in Egypt the name of the Brigade had been changed to 231 Brigade. This was not done without protest being made by Brigadier Smith, O.B.E., who felt that without the Malta association in the title the Brigade would lose something of its individuality and personality. To counteract this, a Brigade sign was designed. It consisted of a white Maltese Cross on the background of a red shield. It was fitting that in this way we should be linked with the hospitallers and templars of old at a time when our defensive role had ended.

The only entry in the official War Diary that relates to planning reads as follows:

"5th May, 1943. Bde. Planning Staff, consisting of Brig. K. P. Smith, O.B.E., Bde. Comd.; Maj. W. E. F. Tuffill (R.W.K.), B.M.; Maj. D. R. Stenhouse (R.E.), D.A.Q.M.G. (Mov.); Capt. F. G. Sadleir (Devon), S.C.; Capt. F. W. Knott (G. Howards), S.C. (Mov.); and Capt. R. T. Gilchrist (King's Own), I.O.; established themselves in offices (rooms 18/21) in Antikhana Buildings, Cairo."

Later they were joined by Capt. H. M. Johnson, who became Staff Captain when Capt. Sadleir was appointed to the post of D.A.A. & Q.M.G. and promoted to the rank of Major, and also Capt. P. J. Hurman, who joined as Brigade R.A.S.C. Officer. On 6th May the main body of the Brigade moved from Mena Camp to the Combined Training Centre at Kabrit on the Suez Canal for training in combined operations.

The secret revealed to selected members the previous month was now made known to all the planning staff. We were going to invade Sicily. The news when received caused no surprise—only quiet satisfaction. Now this secret was the biggest secret in the world, and an attempt was being made to keep it in the worst of all countries for secrets—Egypt. It is difficult to describe the position of Egypt in this war. It is a form of neutrality, a neutrality which is convenient to the Allies and extremely profitable to Egypt. Such a country must be the hotbed of spies and enemy agents. Every form of special training or movement of shipping must be accurately reported. In attempting to preserve our secret we were attempting the impossible.

In fiction, when people desire to plan secretly they choose a site in an oasis or the wilds of a remote Scottish glen. We were allotted a large building in the centre of Cairo. The building itself formed a triangular island. Trams ran down one side of it, a main traffic route down another side, and, almost beyond belief, across the third street was a railway siding, and shunting engines bumped up and down all day. On two sides most of the rooms in our building were overlooked by loftier buildings across the street. The building was surrounded by a tall fence of barbed wire. Outside military policemen patrolled in their red hats. In the doorway members of the Field Security Section stood importantly with their green armbands. It must have been obvious to the most unobservant that " something was up."

The conditions in which we worked in that building are almost beyond description. The exterior of the building was gloomy. The inside was drab and depressing and not overclean. It so happened that most of the time that we were there Egypt was passing through a heat-wave. Work proceeded in an atmosphere of sweat and petrol fumes that rose from the street below. Frequently, to make a remark audible to a fellow-planner the vocal cords were unfairly matched against the clanking of trams, the honking of motor horns and the piercing screams of the shunting engines. The Brigade Commander had a room to himself, but the remainder of the Staff worked together in one small room.

Security was, naturally, of paramount importance, but the person who drafted the Security Regulations for observance by planning staffs did not realize the conditions under which we were to try to apply these regulations. They proved to be a snare for the wary as well as the unwary, and three of the most security-minded on the planning staff found themselves in trouble through no fault of their own.

On one occasion Major Sadleir desired to write a security letter to an officer of another planning staff who was working downstairs in the same building. As it was intended to be delivered personally by hand it was enclosed in one envelope only instead of two as laid down by the regulations. Army Signals, who are usually very efficient, fell down over this and the letter wandered round Egypt, eventually to be opened by a signal master at Alexandria. This official passed the letter to Army, who through Corps administered a " most imperial rocket" demanding an explanation in writing or the instant punishment of the offender. It took all the skill of the Brigade Commander, and the Brigade's principal lawyer and escapologist had to be consulted before Franc Sadleir got out of this one.

Major Stenhouse had offended by dispatching a signal, referring to ships at Suez, marked with the usual security "hokus pokus" from the signal office of the Headquarters of British Troops, Egypt. The crime lay in handing the signal to a clerk in the office, although why such a clerk was not deemed to be in a confidential position and competent to handle the signal was never made clear. A similar demand for vengeance was made. There was no way out of this one and Major Stenhouse was last seen playing for time until he could flee the country with the rest of the expedition. The Intelligence Officer and the Brigade Major also found themselves in great trouble over the matter of a missing photograph.

On 19th May, and at a time when planning had reached a positive and constructive stage, it was announced that Brigadier K. P. Smith, O.B.E., was to leave the Brigade to take up an appointment in England, and that his place was to be taken by Brigadier R. E. Urquhart. In normal times such an event would have shaken the Brigade to its very foundations, but now we had no time to trouble about it. We had undertaken a huge work and that work had to go on. It was only afterwards that we realized how much the Brigade was indebted to Brigadier Smith, O.B.E., for everything he had done during his period of command. His particular genius lay in the toning up and training of fighting men. He had taken over the Brigade in the easy-going days at the end of 1941. Quick to realize the quality of the men under his command, he had ruthlessly started to cut away anything which did not come up to the high standard which he demanded. It was a hard time for most of us, but it was not long before we began to realize Brigadier Smith's conception of what a fighting brigade should be like, and to take pride in it. It was Brigadier Smith who brought the Brigade up to such a standard of training, smartness and general efficiency that called forth the remark from Lord Gort. V.C., that "Malta possessed the finest troops in the world." Though at times a hard man to work for, no one could deny the deep love which he held for his Brigade. He took our troubles on himself and fought our battles against the occasional lack of understanding on the part of higher authority and the more frequent stupidity of unimaginative officialdom and often to the detriment of himself. Brigadier Urquhart had been the G.1 of the famous Highland Division in the successful desert campaigns. A few of the planning staff had met him previously and had been favourably impressed by his qualities. We had no idea at that time what a pillar of strength he was going to prove for the Brigade when it first went into action.

We had been told at a special course of instruction at Kabrit that the bulk of combined operational planning was done on a brigade level, but the full significance of that remark was not realized until later. Anyone who has ever had any experience in military planning will know how difficult it is to maintain an army in the field and to put it into action at the right time and in the right place; yet these are simple matters compared with the mounting of a combined operation. Pause to consider some of the problems involved. In the first place, you are attacking a coast strongly fortified by barbed wire, minefields, coastal defence batteries, and hundreds of carefully concealed concrete pillboxes and fortified positions. In contrast, you yourself are in a small, fragile and very exposed boat. These are the problems of the commander, who is aided by the expert advice of the senior naval officer of landing of the force. Having made his plan, it is now the turn of the staff to prepare orders to implement it.

The force must be equipped for the job on hand. A combined operation requires all sorts of special equipment, and the range runs from scaling-ladders through a long series of anti-malarial stores, such as head-nets, mepachrine tablets, face cream and, finally, to such detail as paper bags in case the men are sick in the landing craft. This by itself would not be considered a formidable task, but, it will be remembered, the battalions had left Malta with very little equipment and they had to be re-equipped from scratch. The position of many of the units which had joined us to form the Brigade Group was little better. This enormous task was to be undertaken for the Brigade by Major Sadleir with the assistance of Capt. Johnson. Franc Sadleir was known in Malta as the most efficient Staff Captain on the Island, but it was only now that he began to show his full powers of hard work and concentration and his uncannily photographic memory for details.

The task of the Brigade Major was equally difficult. In a land operation it is a comparatively simple matter to order a particular unit into action, but in this operation Major Tuffill was entrusted with the task of placing the whole of the Brigade Group and its equipment into ships large enough to sail across the Mediterranean, then embarking them in assault landing craft, and generally seeing that they arrive on the beaches at the right time in the right order and with the right equipment to carry out the Brigade Commander's plan. The problems involved are legion. A certain number of large passenger liners equipped with assault landing craft are allotted to a brigade. These are supplemented by cargo ships for the carriage of stores, and ships specially designed for the carriage and landing of mechanical transport and tanks. The first problem is to decide which men and which stores go into the various ships. With a limited number of ships and thirty or more groups to fit into them, this is no easy matter. Furthermore, a careful distribution of units among ships has to be made in case one or more of the ships are sunk during the voyage.

It would be an easy matter after that if all the ships sailed right up to the high-water mark, and then disembarked their passengers and discharged their cargoes as in the case of a port. But ships opposed by coastal batteries are vulnerable, and they have to lie off a long way from shore. The passage from ship to shore has to be done in small landing craft, and only a limited number of these are carried on the passenger liners. The landing therefore has to be carried out in relays, or, in the special jargon of Combined Ops, in flights. Only a small fraction of the total force can be landed in the first flight, and as these men can expect no other support they must have exactly the right weapons to hand. At this stage in the planning conflicting interests arise between battalions and other units. Some unit commanders require more men in a certain place to carry out the task allotted to them: others require less. So a meeting has to be held, called an " auction," at which the unit commanders make bids to the Brigade Commander for their requirements.

Landing craft will not open out like telescopes. Their sizes are known, but sizes vary considerably. Only a certain number of men and a certain amount of equipment will fit into each craft, and this has to be worked out in great detail. Here the Brigade Major was assisted by Major Stenhouse and Capt. Knott, both expert on movement control, and by Commander Weyman, a naval expert on technical matters. The final task was to load stores into the ships so that they could be off-loaded into landing craft in the order in which they are required. For example—if mortars were required in the early stages of the assault it was useless to have these at the bottom of the hold where they could not be got at until everything else had been moved. Supervision of the loading of the ships was primarily the duty of our movement officers, but the order of loading was very much an operational matter and was the responsibility of the Brigade Major.

The Brigade Intelligence Officer's duties were much simpler. Security was his most important duty at this stage. If the whole enterprise was not to end in costly disaster then surprise must be achieved. Apart from this, the I.O. spent his time pouring over maps and aerial photographs, and absorbing and condensing numerous intelligence summaries dealing with Sicily and the enemy forces with the object of presenting the facts to the Brigade in a precise and more palatable form at a later date.

Condensed in this way, the work of a planning staff may not seem impressive, but there is no point in more detailed description. Either you are an expert in combined operations and you know it all, or you are not—in which case the full details would soon prove tedious reading. Those who do not understand combined operations must accept the bald statement that there is no greater test of organizing ability in the world. How, then, was it accomplished? The answer is *work*—just darned hard work. The routine for the day was to report at the office at 8.30 a.m., take a break of about an hour and a half for lunch, work on until dinner, when a similar break was taken, and then back to work again through the night until 3, 4 or even 5 o'clock on the following morning. This pace the planning staff kept up for three weeks. Antikhana will never be forgotten by those who went through the ordeal. Pictures of Will Tuffill, the Brigade Major, his hair slightly ruffled and a cloud over his usually benevolent face, answering the phone and trying to add figures on an enormous schedule at the same time; of Major Stenhouse, wearing a slightly pained look, trying to fit model paper loads into a deck plan of a model paper boat; of Franc Sadleir falling asleep in his chair during the night and waking up again with a sudden jerk—these memories will live in their minds for ever. Why the planning staff did not fail from sheer mental exhaustion and physical collapse remains a mystery, but they won through and planned a most successful landing.

Meanwhile, at Kabrit, the Brigade was undergoing an intensive course of combined operations training under the supervision of the staff of the Combined Training Centre. We had pretended to train in combined operations in Malta with such equipment as was available, but this was the real thing. Kabrit lies on the end of a peninsula that divides the Great Bitter Lake from the Little Bitter Lake. The Suez Canal, passing through the two Bitter Lakes, lies within a few feet of Kabrit Point. The lakes have all kinds of beaches, and the area is an ideal practice ground for all types of landing operations. The purpose of this training is to accustom the men to the feel of being in a landing craft at sea. They are trained to take up their correct position in the craft with the maximum economy of space, and to disembark speedily, should they come under fire. The correct stowage of guns, mechanical transport, tanks and all types of equipment is also taught. Drivers are practised in driving their vehicles on to and off the craft both from the dry land and through the water. When these first lessons have been learned they are included in tactical schemes—first on a platoon basis, and then later with a battalion or a whole brigade.

At this stage of its history, owing to the concurrent planning in Cairo, the Brigade was almost entirely without Staff officers. Capt. Jennings, the Transport Officer, was acting Brigade Major and Lieut. Turner doubling the duties of the Staff Captain along with his other duties as Camp Commandant and Commander of the Defence Platoon. These two officers had the task of carrying out the orders of the Combined Training Centre for the training of the Brigade, and also endeavouring to comply with the numerous orders received from the planning staff. All the time the other units of the Brigade Group were beginning to assemble round them. With all these administration problems involved it is, of course, impossible for two men to do all these things efficiently, but they are to be congratulated on the effort they made, and there is no doubt that they were every bit as overworked during this period as the party at Antikhana. The battalions, who were accustomed to have an expert on Brigade Staff competent to advise on all matters, showed great tolerance and understanding at this time.

We had left Malta with Brigade Headquarters and three battalions of Infantry. By the end of the training period at Kabrit the following had been added to make up the Brigade Group:

A Brigade Support Company.
A Brigade Group Provost Unit.
A Brigade Group Light Aid Detachment.
A Brigade Group Workshops.
A Brigade Group Postal Unit.
A Squadron and one independent Troop of a Tank Regiment.
A Regiment of Field Artillery.
A Battery of Anti-Tank Guns.
A Battery of Light Anti-Aircraft Guns.
A Field Company of the Royal Engineers.
A Field Ambulance.

A Transport Company of the Royal Army Service Corps.
A Detachment of an Air Support Tentacle.
A Light Section of a Casualty Clearing Station.
A " Nomad " Pigeon Loft.
A Detachment of G.H.Q. Liaison Regiment (Phantom Recce).
And finally a Brick.

Later we were to have other novelties attached, such as interrogators and interpreters, film units, Press representatives and officer observers, Field Security Police and representatives of A.M.G.O.T. (Allied Military Government of Occupied Territories). The purpose of all these units is explained by their names—all except the Brick. A Brick is practically a brigade group in itself. Its function is to make a beach serve in place of a port. Our Brick was built round a battalion of Royal Marines, who provided the labour and stevedore companies. It had a strong signal section, because communications are vital on the beach in the early stages of a landing. It is strong in Engineers, because the beach area has to be cleared of mines and other obstacles, and construction work must be undertaken. It provides its own police for the marking of routes and guarding the prisoner-of-war cage, and it looks after itself with a defence company of Infantry and batteries of heavy A.A. guns and light A.A. guns.

The training at Kabrit ended with a Brigade exercise called " Duchess," and the planning staff at Cairo was recalled to take part. For Brigade Staff the exercise " Duchess " had more air of reality than the real thing itself, which took place later. The remainder of the Brigade Group embarked on the landing craft from the beaches, and then crossed the lake and made their " exercise " assault on the opposite shore, but Brigade Headquarters embarked from H.M.S. *Keren,* the headquarters ship which had anchored in the Canal for the real assault. It was a very dark night, and about thirty minutes before zero hour we took up action positions in the operations room. A long wait followed, until finally an observer outside reported tracer being fired on the beaches, and we knew that the first flights had made contact with the enemy. Then events followed swiftly, until a light signal from the beach was observed signifying success of one of the battalions, and the reserve battalion was ordered in to exploit the success on that beach. Finally Headquarters themselves made the long journey across the dark lake.

Apart from getting the feel of the thing, this exercise was of great value, because as far as possible the conditions which we would meet in Sicily were reproduced on the ground, and many lessons were learned and faults in the planning corrected. Brigadier Urquhart took part in the exercise as a spectator only. It was his first chance of watching his Brigade Group in a mock action. For the purpose of the scheme the part of the Brigade Commander was played by Lieut.-Colonel Duke, of the C.T.C.

On 24th May and two days after the end of exercise " Duchess," the Brigade Group moved to camp at Fayid, near Geniefa. All the planning staff were now finally recalled from Antikhana, but planning had to go on. At Antikhana there had at least been well-equipped offices, but now there was nothing but a tent in the sand and a depressing lack of accommodation stores. Turned-up ammunition boxes served as chairs, and the Intelligence Officer complained bitterly that he was expected to make traces and sketch maps on a table constructed of corrugated iron.

With the round-up of the last German in North Africa it became clear that desert fighting had ended for this war. It caused some surprise, therefore, when the Brigade Commander announced that he was going to put the Brigade through a four-day exercise of " hard living " in the desert. The exercise commenced on the 1st and ended on the morning of the 5th May, and was called exercise " Nomad." It was in four phases. The first phase was a move to a concentration area and practice living in bivouac. The second phase was a move to relieve the imaginary troops in forward areas and to make contact with the enemy. The third phase consisted of intensive night patrolling. Phases two and three were carried out by the Hampshires and Dorsets. The final phase was a night attack by the Devons, supported by tanks and artillery. Of all the pre-invasion exercises " Nomad " was probably the most instructive. It certainly gave most of us our first experience of sleeping in holes in the sand, of continued exposure to the fierce Egyptian sun, and strict rationing of water, on the scale of half a gallon a day for all purposes. For troops whose training had completely lacked mobility, this was a stiff task, but afterwards Brigadier Urquhart expressed himself well satisfied, which from a man of his experience in desert warfare was high praise indeed.

Meanwhile planning continued. It was a completely crazy existence. The Brigade Major would give out orders in the desert for an " exercise " attack and then turn immediately to some problem connected with landing tables for the real assault. Franc Sadleir would tackle some problem about water supply for our desert scheme and at the back of his mind would be some problem connected with a return of medical stores required in Sicily. Trying to maintain security was reducing the I.O. to a state of neurosis. All his secrets were kept in a large wooden box. This box could only be opened when everyone else had been " shooed " out of the tent. The I.O. lived with that box for weeks. It was like Mary's little lamb, for everywhere the I.O. went the box was sure to go.

An exercise called " Brightling " was due to commence on 9th May and was to last about eight days. " Brightling " was to be a full-scale exercise, and it was designed to reproduce the real assault in minute detail. Planning the real and the imaginary at the same time led to some confusion, but in view of the magnitude of the planning and the speed at which it had to be done, the general standard of efficiency was remarkable.

It only required exercise " Brightling " to give the final touches of unreality to the period. For this exercise the Brigade Group embarked on H.M.S. *Keren*, s.s. *Strathnever* and s.s. *Otranto* at Suez on 9th and 10th June. The general scheme was to sail down to Safaga on the Red Sea, carry out a signal exercise, follow this on the next day by a full-scale exercise on the " Duchess " pattern, and then return to Suez. A strenuous exercise in the Red Sea in June was not a pleasing prospect to most of us, but we need not have worried, for the weather had decreed that " Brightling " should be a pleasure cruise. There was a cool breeze blowing when we embarked at Suez, but on the first day out Capt. The Lord Ashbourne, our S.N.O.L. (Senior Naval Officer Landing), announced that it was blowing a gale at Safaga and that the exercise would have to wait until the wind subsided, as he dare not risk his landing craft in the rough seas.

The seas never did subside—at least not in the Red Sea. We lay off Safaga for two days and viewed with interest through binoculars the complicated system of barbed wire and fortifications the " exercise " enemy had prepared to discomfort our landing. Then it was suggested that Jemsa Bay would be a more sheltered place, so we sailed northwards to this bay, which is practically in the Gulf of Suez, followed by the " exercise " enemy on shore. The unfortunate troops acting as enemy must have had a very bad time. Theirs was only a " stooge " job at best, but to wander up and down the coast of Africa preparing defences while we made up our minds where to land must have been most discouraging. What they really thought of us must have been well worth listening to.

Jemsa was no better than Safaga for a landing, and by now

the exercise had begun to take on the appearance of a farce. When we were told that positive information had been received that the seas were calm enough at Aqaba for a landing and that we were going to sail up the gulf, no one really believed it.

Soldiers are much-travelled people, but I doubt if any one of us had ever been to Aqaba before. The small town lies at the head of the long Gulf of Aqaba. This gulf has some great depths in it, for it is in the line of that peculiar rift in the earth's surface which starts at the Dead Sea and ends on the coast of Africa. On one side the mountains of Saudi Arabia tower above it; on the other side the mountains of Sinai with all their Biblical associations. Aqaba was used by Lawrence of Arabia as a base in the First World War. The place is also unique because it is the junction of the boundaries of four countries and two continents.

Aqaba had been used as the training ground of another assaulting force and we had passed their returning convoy as we sailed up the gulf. The defences on the ground were quickly altered, and the enemy redisposed to meet our requirements, and at 3 a.m. on 16th May the landing exercise "Brightling" commenced. It was all over by 10 a.m. and all the troops were re-embarked by midday. The ships immediately up-anchored and sailed back to Suez, where they arrived the following day.

The exercise at Aqaba went like clockwork, because we had by now become expert in combined operations. Exercise "Brightling" was also valuable because it accustomed the men to getting into the landing craft from the liners that were going to carry them to Sicily. Everyone, except the planning staff, who carried on their labours as usual, had a well-earned rest.

We were by now fully trained combined operators, and the remainder of the time at Fayid Camp was devoted to putting the finishing touches to the planning and to "briefing." The intelligence supplied by Corps and Army from the very start of the planning to the end of the campaign was of the very highest order, and at this stage nothing was spared which would make the task of the assaulting troops easier. To illustrate the instructions given by commanding officers, large-scale models were produced of the objective, in which every house, every wall and tree was faithfully reproduced. These were supplemented by all types of aerial photographs—stereoscopic pairs to bring out in relief camouflaged trenches and gun positions—huge enlargements giving a bird's-eye view over the whole area—and oblique snapshots of the beaches taken from such a low altitude that the airman who secured them must have been in grave peril of his life.

It was now the turn of the Intelligence Officer to play his part and to disgorge some of the many facts which he had absorbed during the past two months. Party after party stood round those models and photographs each day until all the senior officers in the Brigade Group had been thoroughly instructed in the nature and position of enemy defences, and the general topography of the area.

During the last few days in Egypt the Corps Commander and General Montgomery visited us and delivered lectures.

" My technique of battle," said " Monty," " is to deprive the enemy of the initiative and make him dance to my tune."

All that remained now was to see that every bit of equipment was in the right place, and that everyone carried the right kit for the job. In normal kit a soldier is dressed up like a Christmas tree, but for a combined operation he carries in addition an entrenching tool, a special assault respirator, which is smaller but more of a nuisance than the ordinary type, and every pouch and haversack bulges with reserve ammunition and spare barrels for Bren guns. On top of all this, he has to manage somehow to drape a life-jacket. When leaving Fayid for the last time, a busy officer was passing down the train checking the contents of each truck. " Are there any light ack-ack in there? " he shouted at one truck. " No," came the immediate answer, " but there are some bloody heavy infantry."

Advance parties left for Suez on the 27th of the month, and the main body of the Brigade Group embarked on our old friends *Keren, Strathnever* and *Otranto* at Suez on the 29th. The period of planning and the period of pretence was over. The curtain was up for the real show.

The period of planning had been the ordeal and the triumph of the Brigade planning staff, but it should not be imagined that they were the only planners concerned. Planning started with the Army and went right down to platoons, but it reached its height of intensity at Brigade level. The battalions and other units in the Brigade Group had their own immense problems of administration and organization, and throughout the whole of this period they were indifferently served by an overworked Brigade Staff. Frequently they were called upon to move the whole battalion to a new camp or on an exercise at a few hours' notice; lengthy returns had to be rendered immediately, and transport and new equipment were showered on them like rain from heaven. All this they tolerated without signs of irritation, but undoubtedly their finest contribution was the deep and sympathetic understanding of the trials of the Staff.

On the last day in May the convoy sailed from Suez. As we sailed up the Suez Canal for the last time and passed the Combined Training Centre at Kabrit, Major de Coursay Ireland, of the Brick, made the following signal: "Hail, Alma Mater. From 3,000 old boys."

The journey to Sicily was a pleasure cruise. Certainly that will be the impression of most officers and men who travelled in the *Keren*, the Headquarters ship. An impartial observer would never have believed that here were men of set purpose journeying with the intention of making the first big-scale forcible entry on to enemy soil. A signal had been received from high Army quarters stating that no alcoholic drink would be consumed on the voyage, but the *Keren*, being a naval ship under command of the Senior Service, tactfully decided to ignore this, and business in the bar went on as usual. While we were in the Canal zone and black-out did not matter, cinema shows were given nightly on deck. On arrival at Port Said the whole of the Brigade Group was dispatched on a route march along the beaches, followed by a bathe in the surf. Alongside the ship keen water-polo matches were played between Army and Navy teams. Later in the voyage a boxing contest was organized and nightly fierce battles were fought on the deck hockey pitch—a pastime far more dangerous than fighting Italians. For those who liked the quieter life there were the resources of the ship's library and the comforts of gin and tobacco at incredibly cheap prices.

Practices of boat stations and action stations were cut to a minimum. It must not be imagined from this that there was any slackness or feeling of detachment on board. The officers who sailed the ship knew their job thoroughly. They realized that the crews under their command and every man on board knew their job also, and they had the good sense to leave it at that—without any of the fuss or display that lesser men would have demanded.

The secret of our destination had been known to the planning staff for three months. Photographs and models of our objective had been on display to officers for a week before sailing. The name of the place was carefully concealed, but there must have been very few officers who could not have made a very shrewd guess at it. The men had been kept completely in the dark. Now, as we left Port Said, our final port of call, the secret was made known to all. Photographs and models were on display and the Brigade Intelligence Section painted the decks with sketches of the beaches, the Brigade objectives, maps of Sicily and a plan of the beach maintenance area, until the *Keren* began to look like an art gallery—and groups of men wandered from picture to picture like connoisseurs. Lectures were given on every imaginable subject which might help the operation. Some enthusiasts even started German and Italian lessons. Photographs of the beaches and explanatory intelligence summaries were handed to all officers. Every man was given an excellent little booklet called " The Soldier's Guide to Sicily." The two extracts from this book that attracted the most attention read as follows:

" Fruit and nuts, oranges, lemons, almonds and pistachios are very plentiful. Wine, especially Marsala, is the popular drink. Grapes or candied orange and lemon peel are produced for dessert "; and

" The Sicilian is still, however, well known for his extreme jealousy in so far as his womenfolk are concerned, and in a crisis still resorts to the dagger."

It began to occur to the men that in such a country flowing with milk and honey and containing women worth the hazard of a dagger duel, there was something in this invasion business after all.

And so in slow majesty the great convoy of thirty liners sailed across the blue waters of the Mediterranean. Far away, other convoys of equal size were converging on the same focal point. Sicily had become a cynosure for all eyes.

On our last full day at sea out of the sun-kissed mist of the distant horizon loomed the remainder of our attendant craft. Cargo ships, tank landing craft, destroyers and motor speed launches—they had sailed from different ports, and now seemed to fill all the unoccupied spaces in the sea as they joined the Armada.

About midday the following signal was received from Field-Marshal Lord Gort, V.C., from Malta:

" The Service Commanders, the Lieutenant-Governor and myself all send you our heartfelt good wishes.

" The 1st Malta Brigade—the title by which we will always remember you—is very much in our thoughts on the eve of the date of battles to come which are sure to discomfort the enemy on his own soil.

" Never shall good fortune desert the fighting men of Devonshire, Hampshire and Dorsetshire.

" This constitutes our fervent prayer.

" May victory be yours."

That evening just before sunset the black mass of Mount Etna became visible off the starboard bow. Sicily lay ahead. The beliefs of the private soldier die hard. Despite all our special training, despite all our planning and our exercises at sea, there were still some who had actually to see Sicily before they were finally convinced that we were *not* going home.

CHAPTER III

THE LANDING

THE PLAN FOR THE LANDING was made by Brigadier Smith and was adopted by Brigadier Urquhart practically *in toto*. XXX Corps had given orders that we should make an assault near a village called Marsamemi on the eastern coast of Sicily. Marsamemi is on the Pachino Peninsula, which forms the south-eastern extremity of the island. The town of Pachino is situated about two miles south-west of Marsamemi. The area that the Brigade was ordered to capture and hold consisted of three miles of coastline and land inwards to an average depth of about two miles.

Very full information had been received about this area from intelligence sources. We knew that the village of Marsamemi lay on a headland in the centre of this strip of coastline, and that it had a population of about 700. We knew that the principal industry of Marsamemi was tunny fishing, and that the area as a whole was devoted to the growing of vines and production of wine. Any slight inaccuracy on a map could easily be corrected by study of aerial photographs. Immediately to the south of Marsamemi was a bay a thousand yards in length, which itself split up into three smaller bays. The centre of these three smaller bays was fouled by many rocks and deemed to be unsuitable for landing. The other two bays offered prospects of a good landing for all types of craft, and these were selected after consultation with our naval advisers. From north to south they were named " Amber " and " Red " Beach respectively.

Intelligence reports stated that the enemy troops centred on Pachino, and guarding the peninsula, did not exceed a coastal battalion and a machine-gun battalion. The nearest Italian field force was the Napoli Division, which was known to be some distance inland. The only troops capable of making a counter-attack were at Rosolini, approximately twelve miles away. Of the German forces little was known except that there were elements of two or possibly three divisions somewhere in the island. These German forces were thought to be armoured. The local enemy defences had been pin-pointed by aerial photography. They comprised a belt of wire running the whole length of the beaches, a forward defensive line of emplacements and concrete pillboxes at an average interval of 500 yards, and a few defended localities inland sited in depth. The only formidable military opposition appeared likely to come from a gun position of four medium guns which had been located at a distance of approximately two miles inland. Topographically this area was ideal. An excellent lateral road ran between Marsamemi and Pachino, and at least three other possible roads for transport led away from the beaches to the general line of exploitation inland. The country rose in gentle undulations to a height of about 150 feet. Vineyards, carob trees and olive trees offered excellent cover for attacking troops and dispersal of vehicles. Running parallel to the beach at a distance of approximately 500 yards was a single-track railway line.

With all the other inevitable difficulties of combined operations to contend with, Brigadier Smith had determined that the plan of assault should be as simple as possible. Briefly, it consisted of surprise attacks on the two beaches from the flanks, with the object of taking the enemy defences on the beaches from the rear. With the beaches securely in our hands, the remainder of the troops of two battalions were to come through and exploit by bounds on the left and right halves of the sector respectively. The railway line was to be used as a mark, easily distinguishable in the dark, for one of these bounds. A sufficient bridgehead having been secured, the third battalion was then to land and make an attack on the gun position, supported by tanks and light artillery (3.7 howitzers). On the successful completion of this attack the advance of the other two battalions was to continue until the final stage was reached, when all three battalions would be disposed along the perimeter of the allotted area. Meantime the Brick were to carry on with unloading supplies and building up a maintenance area.

The journey from Port Said to the shores of Sicily had been quite uneventful, and to everyone's surprise there had been no interference from aircraft, submarines or surface vessels. The weather, too, had been favourable, but on the night of 9th July the wind rose and the ships began to rock on a heavy swell. This continued throughout the night, but fortunately eased slightly

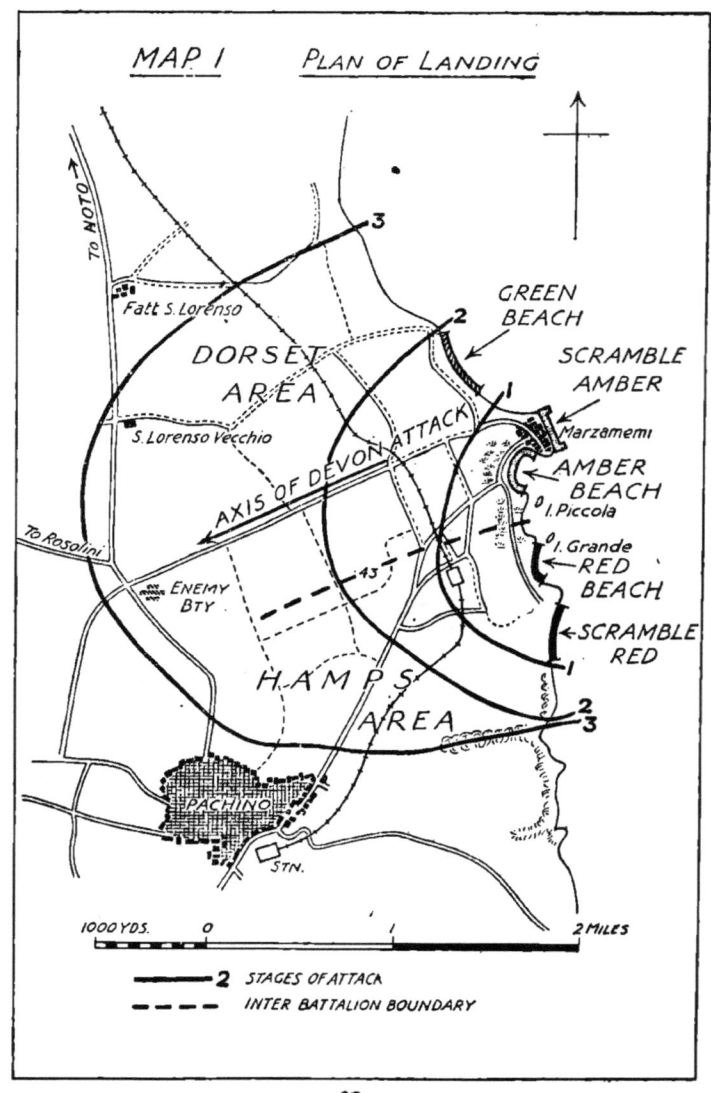

before the troops were to embark into the landing craft. At 0245 hrs. the landing craft left for the beaches. They had been committed to their tasks and as far as Brigade Headquarters were concerned no further control of the battle was possible until Headquarters were established on shore. It was a dark night, and all that could be seen was a heavy air raid in progress in the Catania and Siracusa areas, and the gunboat to the south of the island firing salvo after salvo.

Eventually, at about 0400 hrs., Very-light signals were seen which indicated that the beaches had been captured by the Hampshires and Dorsets, and later this was confirmed by code words received over the wireless. At 0500 hrs. serial No. 35 (an L.C.P.R.) containing Brigade Tac. H.Q., consisting of the Brigade Commander, Brigade I.O. and selected intelligence and signal personnel, left the *Keren* for the beaches. The swell had diminished slightly, but the sea was still rough, and those who were unfortunate to be well forward were drenched by the spray coming over the bows. The naval rating steering the boat did not appear certain of his bearings, and had it not been for the directions given by the Brigade Commander and Brigade I.O., the Tac. H.Q. might well have missed the island altogether, as there was a strong current running to the south.

Eventually it was light enough to see land and to pick out our particular beaches from the rest of the Sicilian mainland. The sea was a mass of shipping, with hundreds of small boats between the liners and the shore. The Dutch sloops *Flores* and *Soemba,* which had escorted our convoy, were firing salvos directed at the coastal defence battery in our area. This coastal defence battery was firing into the sea, and several rounds fell near the Brigadier's craft. A mortar also appeared to be firing into the sea. The action of this coastal defence battery was one of the most astonishing things of the campaign. Had the guns been directed on to the beaches they would have undoubtedly done great damage and caused confusion. As it was, the shells were falling harmlessly into the sea, and apart from one lucky hit which caused no loss of life no damage was done. More frightening were two M.E.109's which were circling low and machine-gunning craft.

The landing on " Amber " beach was completely " dry "— that is, one was able to step directly from ship to shore. At this stage and later the landing seemed to lack reality. We had expected bullet-swept beaches, but here were a peaceful little bay and village, and only occasionally a shell went overhead, or a sniper fired an isolated shot. At 0600 hrs. Brigade H.Q. established themselves within 100 yards of the beach at Marsamemi. At 0730 hrs. the coastal defence battery was knocked out by our supporting guns, and by 0800 hrs. Brigade H.Q. had regained sufficient control of the battle to ascertain that the two assaulting battalions had reached the line of the second objective, and in some cases were even beyond this line.

Many people who made the landing after the assaulting troops received the impression that the assault and capture of the beaches had been easy, but this was far from being the case. All the troops in the assaulting craft had a very rough voyage, and the paper bags provided in case of sea-sickness circulated freely. As in the Brigade Commander's craft, many were soaked to the skin by the water which was shipped. Many craft, owing to the indifferent navigation of the crews, had difficulty in finding the beaches. The second flight of the Hampshires' attack, which contained the Commanding Officer's landing craft and five other landing craft, did not make the rendezvous with the rest of the landing squadron. The result was that they sailed on their own, and it was not until they saw the green success signal, fired by the Dorsets, that they realized that they were positioned well to the north of our beaches. Eventually they discovered that the beach on which they were to have landed was still under fire and they landed on the beach known as "Scramble Red." No. 17 Platoon of the Hampshires, which should have been the left flank and on the extreme south, were landed well to the north of all the beaches, and had to cross through the Dorsets' area before making contact with the remainder of the company. The craft which contained the Second-in-Command of the Dorsets found land several miles to the south and had a long voyage before reaching the correct beaches.

The Italian coastal defence troops on this sector were in strong fortified positions, and in many cases kept on firing and sniping after our troops had gone by. Our troops went for these enemy positions "flat out" as soon as they were located, and many were the deeds of valour and daring done in the darkness and half-light. For example, there were Capt. A. P. Boyd and Cpl. Higgins, of the Hampshires, who, on landing, found themselves on a beach swept by fire from an enemy pillbox. There was no time to cut the double apron wire fence which confronted them, and with a fine disregard for any mines that might have been lying around they flung themselves bodily across the obstacle to make a path for the following troops. Capt. Boyd was wounded, but he still carried on.

The Hampshire company, commanded by Capt. A. K. Guest,

was delayed, and it was light before it landed. In full light Capt. Guest led a succession of assaults against enemy strong-points, and himself knocked out one of these posts with the assistance of a few men of his Company H.Q.

Then there was the heroic action of Lieut. J. D. Le Brecht, of the Hampshire Regiment, who, observing his own troops and men of the Dorset battalion to be under fire from buildings in the rear, attacked these buildings with three men, killing several of the enemy and capturing 2 officers and 35 other ranks. He also was wounded but carried on.

Then there was the individual effort of Sergt. W. Parris, of the Hampshire Regiment, who stalked an enemy pillbox single-handed with hand grenades and killed several of the occupants.

The landing of the Dorset battalion was somewhat easier, but they also had their acts of gallantry. Capt. A. C. W. Martin, a company commander, had an extremely difficult role to perform. His was the landing on the extreme right flank. It comprised the scrambling ashore on a rocky part of the coast, climbing over a sea wall 6 feet high, clearing the village of Marsamemi, and outflanking " Amber " beach to secure a passage for the rest of the battalion. All this he did with skill and cool courage, and in the village he personally led an attack against a strong enemy pillbox.

Sergt. G. Wilson, of the Dorsets, also took part in the clearing of the village. He took over command when his platoon commander was wounded, and led the final assault on two enemy machine-gun posts at the north end of the village. At the point of the bayonet these posts were attacked and all the occupants killed.

There were also several cases of Dorset men who were wounded in the early part of the assault yet carried on with their duties until they were compelled by orders of an officer or sheer exhaustion to seek medical aid.

The Gunners also had their adventures. One landing craft containing a section of 3.7 howitzers was unable to land on " Red " beach owing to enemy fire. On the journey round to " Amber " beach it received a direct hit from a shell, but the guns were landed successfully. As it left the beach to return to the ship it received another direct hit and was sunk.

The 165 Field Regiment, R.A., and the Dutch gunboats both claimed to have knocked out the Italian coastal defence battery. Lieut. Lewis, who directed the fire from the gunboats, had established his O.P. well forward of the most advanced Hampshire platoon. Shortly after the Dutch sloops opened fire, they registered three direct hits on the battery almost in succession. The battery was silenced, and Lieut. Lewis, forgetting his exposed position, pranced wildly about excitedly gesticulating and explaining to anyone willing to listen what perfect shots they were.

The 165 Field Regiment, R.A., put their light howitzers ashore at great speed, and at 0730 hrs., shortly after they had commenced firing, the opposing battery went out of action. The credit therefore for destroying this enemy battery so quickly must be shared jointly by the Army and the Navy.

The Devons were the reserve battalion and took no part in the assault on the beaches. They had, however, to wait for the success of the other two battalions before they could land, and some of the men were as long as five hours in the landing craft. Most of them were sea-sick.

The task of the Devons was to move through the bridgehead established by the Hampshires and Dorsets and to make an attack on the coastal defence battery supported by the first Sherman tanks to land.

In addition, they had been ordered to give support to the landing battalions with mortars and machine guns landed early in the operation on two small islands a few yards from the shore. On one of these islands there was a small chalet, the property of an Italian professor, who spent his summer holidays there— or so the Intelligence said. Rumour had added a charming daughter, who always visited her father in July. On arrival at the beaches it was noticed that the chalet had had a direct hit from previous bombing, but there was no time to speculate on the fate of the lovely daughter.

The Devons quickly reached their assembly area without incident, except for some very poor quality sniping from the rear. As the enemy coastal defence battery had already received attention from the guns, Major Hastings, with " A " Company, had no difficulty in taking the position and capturing there three 175-mm. guns, one field gun and a large quantity of stores and ammunition.

" A " and " B " Companies of the Devons then continued to advance towards a wooded ridge beyond the battery from where machine-gun and rifle fire was observed to be coming. It proved to be held by Italians, who fired wildly until our troops approached, and then surrendered in large numbers.

By this time it was noon, and the Brigade had captured the whole of the allotted area, except for the Dorsets, who were held back on the right flank by a counter-attack by tanks which

THE NAVY DOES IT AGAIN.

The convoy off the Sicilian Beaches with H.M.S. Keren, Headquarters ship of the Malta Brigade, in the background.

[Crown Copyright Reserved

was just developing. This counter-attack took up all the early part of the afternoon. It was made by French M.35 tanks manned by Italians from Rosolini. The existence and composition of this force had been known in advance, and the counter-attack came in exactly at the time and place expected. The result was that the attacking tanks were met by Sherman tanks and most of the Brigade Group's 17-pounder and 6-pounder anti-tank guns. Despite this, the attack was pressed home strongly, but the Italians had no chance. It is worth noting, however, that this was the only counter-attack made against us by the Italians throughout the campaign, and in view of the heavy odds against them was conducted with great gallantry. Few people in the area knew anything about this tank battle which was taking place in the wooded country a mile ahead.

And so by about 1600 hrs. the Brigade had carried out all its allotted tasks. The beaches had been assaulted, the covering positions captured, and the expected counter attack repulsed. All that remained now was to dispatch a swift-moving column northwards to contact XIII Corps, whose troops had landed in the Avola area.

The 10th July was a great day for the Brigade Group. The Navy conducted the whole of our forces to the beaches of Sicily almost without loss, and because of their wonderful work and organization the Brigade had been given a fine start. Capt. The Lord Ashbourne, who commanded our naval force, and all the officers and men under his command had done a magnificent job of work from the start of the planning up to the time of parting on the beaches.

The plan for the capture of the beaches and covering positions had proved to be a good one. The landing was a triumph for the planning staff. Everything which they had laid down in their orders was carried out without a hitch, and the speed of the discharging of stores exceeded all expectations. The success in that day's fighting justified all the hard training and exercises that had preceded it. It was a particularly triumphant day for the Intelligence. The enemy positions were found to be where they had been stated to be. The enemy troops belonged to units the identities of which had previously been forecast, and the enemy counter-attack had come in at exactly the time and place predicted. The element of surprise was entirely on our side. Furthermore, the suddenness and speed of our attack had resulted in the capture of many sets of maps, traces and documents and these were to prove of great value later in the campaign.

CHAPTER IV

THE ROAD TO NOTO

IT WAS PART OF THE CORPS PLAN that 231 Brigade should, after establishing themselves firmly on the land, patrol to and make contact with XIII Corps, who had landed about thirteen miles farther north. Because of this, much intelligence work had been put into the study of the route and topography. A prisoner had been captured who must have travelled this road many times, for he was able to describe it yard by yard, and a very valuable report was compiled from his disclosures. The main obstacle on the road to Noto was the River Tellaro. This river contained water even in mid-summer and it ran between steep built-up banks, and on either side of it was a network of canals and irrigation ditches. There was only one bridge where the road crossed the river: otherwise a long deviation had to be made along tracks and third-class roads. The road from the south as it approached the river was flat and very exposed. Beyond the river to the north, however, the ground rose steeply, and several pillboxes and prepared positions had been spotted. All this the aerial photographic interpreters told us well in advance.

Provided the bridge was demolished the place was, of course, a perfect obstacle. Tanks and vehicles could not have got across without the Engineers first constructing a bridge, which would prove a long and expensive business if they were exposed to enemy fire. It was not even an attractive objective for the Infantry, for the advantage appeared to be entirely with the defence. Brigadier Urquhart decided to solve the problem by a rapid advance of a mobile column with the object of taking the enemy by surprise before they had the opportunity to demolish the bridge. The Devons were ordered to provide one company to lead this mobile column, and they were to have the support of the carriers from the Dorsets, tanks from 46 R.T.R. and anti-tank guns from 300 Anti-Tank Battery.

It had not yet been decided, while we were on board the *Keren,* which of the Devon companies was going to undertake this task, and all the Devon commanders had to be put in the Intelligence picture. One evening aboard ship the Brigade I.O. gave a travel talk, which the Devons themselves had billed " The Road to Noto." It was as if Kipling had been asked to give a talk on " The Road to Mandalay " with this difference, that neither the lecturer nor the audience had ever seen the place under discussion.

At 1800 hrs. on 10th July the Brigade Commander held a conference at Brigade H.Q. at which he informed the assembled unit commanders that the Brigade had lost its independent role and had now come under command of the 51st (Highland) Division. The Brigade was ordered to move to Noto immediately, followed by the 153rd Brigade of the Highland Division. The other two brigades of the Highland Division were to advance to Noto, by the longer routes via Rosolini. For 231 Brigade the order of move was as follows: 2 Devon, 1 Hamps, Bde. H.Q. and 1 Dorset.

For the majority of the men in the Brigade the move to Noto proved unspectacular. A heavy air raid was in progress over the Marsamemi beaches as we left, and we were not sorry to get away from that area and leave that part of the battle to our 352 L.A.A. Battery, which had every gun in action. The evening was cool, and the air was later to turn quite cold in the small hours. Although there was a bright moon, progress was slow owing to the congestion of traffic on the road. About midnight most units halted to snatch a few hours' rest.

By dawn it became known that the advance by the Devons had been most successful. They had captured a strong enemy position, secured the crossing of the River Tellaro, and were holding positions on the high ground to the north. The Hampshires and Dorsets were ordered to pass through the Devons and to take up positions to the north and north-west of Noto. Brigade H.Q. followed up and established themselves near the bridge where the main road crosses the River Asinaro on the south-east side of Noto, and later the Devons established themselves in approximately the same position.

The story of the road to Noto told in this way, as it might well be by anyone who was not with the forward troops, appears dull and uninteresting. Let the story now be told, therefore, as it appeared to the men of " D " Company, 2nd Devonshire Regiment, who were selected to lead the advance. " D " Company had with them a carrier platoon, a troop of Sherman tanks and a troop of anti-tank guns. All were under the command of Major Biggart.

Soon after the start the mobile column came under fire from a machine-gun post and two light tanks. Sergt. Willis, with No. 18 Platoon, dealt with the post by working round to a flank and then rushing it and throwing hand grenades. Their bag was 85 prisoners, 2 Breda guns and 7 heavy machine guns. The two light tanks were knocked out by the Shermans, and the column continued its advance.

From then onwards for the next few miles "D" Company kept up a most satisfactory rate of advance. This was done by "ferrying" two platoons forward on carriers while the other platoons rode on the tanks.

About half-way to the River Tellaro the leading platoon noticed a large party of Italian troops on the right of the road and engaged them with their Bren guns, while Capt. Eteson took his carriers down the road to try to cut them off. On rounding the next bend, however, he immediately came under fire from an anti-tank gun which was firing straight down the road. He withdrew his carriers and went to seek the assistance of Lieut. Clark, who was close behind with his mortars. Lieut. Clark was going forward to reconnoitre when his party came under fire from a large farm standing back from the road on their left. Lieut. Clark, with Sergt. Jeffery and Ptes. Kuhn and Palmer, worked his way up to this farm, which he found to be a large rambling building with numerous out-houses. They were standing in the courtyard trying to spot the sniper's hide-out when a sudden burst of light-automatic fire made them all dive for the nearest doorway. Peering out through a window, Lieut. Clark caught sight of a cleverly camouflaged observation post built amongst the branches of a tall tree, and it was from this that the fire was coming. Realizing that the O.P. would probably be armoured and that something more than light-arms fire would be required, he managed to get out of the farm and to direct the fire of a tank on to it. One burst of fire from the tank and the O.P. disappeared in a cloud of smoke, accompanied by the explosions of numerous blue and yellow flares. After that there was no more sniping.

Meanwhile, Major Biggart had made his plan for dealing with the enemy position along the road. Two of the Shermans reported that they could give covering fire, and C.S.M. Bollam with three other N.C.Os. had managed to get into a position from which they could engage the enemy frontally. Lieut. J. D. Campbell, accompanied by Lieut. J. F. H. Arundell, then took two platoons round the left flank, and as soon as they got near enough they charged the post and captured it. To their surprise, as they approached, they heard English voices shouting "Come on in now, you've got them." The voices belonged to two British paratroopers who had been dropped in the sea by mistake the night before, and had been captured after swimming ashore. This little action produced a haul of 9 anti-tank guns, 2 heavy machine guns and 120 prisoners.

Whilst "D" Company reorganized, "A" Company, under

Major Hastings, took the lead and continued the advance. The country now became more wooded and enclosed, which slowed down the rate of advance owing to the necessity for searching the ground on each side of the road, and examining buildings. The crossing of the River Tellaro was finally reached at 0210 hrs. on 11th July, and all were relieved to find the bridge intact.

" A " Company immediately pressed forward to attack the covering positions which were known to exist on the high ground beyond the river and to the west of the road, but they met with little opposition. Capt. Eteson then took a carrier patrol up to the high ground north of the river which was the battalion objective, and as no enemy showed themselves the battalion advanced and occupied it. " C " and " B " Companies were now overlooking Noto, " D " Company were in reserve about halfway down the hill, and " A " Company remained in the position they had captured.

During the occupation of this area there was an amusing incident. No. 16 Platoon of " D " Company had been allotted their locality and were preparing to dig themselves in. Two of the men, finding that someone else had done the job for them, called out, " There is no need to dig here, Sergeant; there are slit trenches here already." The trenches were partially covered with straw, and when this was removed out came 3 Italian officers and 25 men, who were only too anxious to surrender. That was not all; further investigation revealed a partially constructed concrete post with an anti-tank gun and a Breda, both loaded and pointing straight down the road up which the battalion had advanced a short time before. No. 16 Platoon added the Breda to their armament and acquired a donkey and cart as transport, but the subsequent rapid rate of advance proved too much for the donkey, and the gun had to be reluctantly abandoned. The Devons had now been engaged in active operations for thirty hours without stopping. They had made an uncomfortable landing and advanced over thirteen miles into enemy territory. It was a fine effort of endurance on the part of all ranks.

The rapid advance to Noto and the securing of the River Tellaro were more than a personal triumph for the 2nd Bn. The Devonshire Regiment. It was a move of the greatest strategical importance. By bringing troops into the Noto area it provided XIII Corps with a firm base from which to strike northwards against Catania and the airfields at Gerbini. It relieved the whole of XXX Corps from a state of congestion in the restricted area of the Pachino Peninsula. Even after this outlet had been provided the Canadians were squeezed out of the early part of the campaign by the Highland Division on the right and the Americans on the left. Had 231 Brigade and the Highland Division not secured this outlet to the north and been able to start the long movement which went via Palazzolo, Vizzini and Caltagirone and which was only to turn when Enna had been reached, the whole campaign might well have been prolonged by several weeks.

CHAPTER V

ON TO VIZZINI

EARLY IN THE MORNING OF 11TH JULY the Brigade Group had settled into defensive positions round Noto. At that time it was thought that the role of the Brigade and of the Highland Division was to be a further move northwards to the Avola area, in order to relieve troops of XIII Corps for an attack against Catania. By this time the port of Syracuse had been captured and the original Army plan of a drive along the east coast of Sicily to Messina appeared as if it was going well and likely to be successful ahead of schedule.

That morning the Brigade Commander met the General commanding the Highland Division on the road a few miles south of Noto. During the conference General Montgomery rode up in a duck. A duck is rather like a large lifeboat on wheels. It is an extraordinary sight to see in a country lane. " Monty " was in great spirits and seemed delighted with his vehicle. He stood in the bows—like a Viking—and acknowledged the salutes of the soldiers as he passed. With the Army Commander was Lord Louis Mountbatten, Chief of Combined Operations. They were making their way to Syracuse.

About midday two platoons of the Dorsets, the carriers of the Hampshires, the 300 Anti-Tank Battery less one troop, and a light section of the Field Ambulance came under the command of " Harpoon Force." This force consisted of the 23rd Armoured Brigade under the command of Brigadier Richards, and supporting artillery. Its task was to clear any opposition that might remain in the Rosolini area and to push forward in a north-westerly direction exploiting success whenever possible.

Except for the troops engaged with Harpoon Force, the Brigade Group remained in defensive positions in the Noto area for twenty-four hurs. On the morning of the 12th the two Dorset platoons with Harpoon Force were known to be making good progress towards Palazzolo along the most southerly of the two roads that lead north-west from Noto. About midday the remainder of the Brigade Group were ordered to follow up. The Devons led on the southern road, followed by Brigade H.Q. and the Dorsets, while the Hampshires moved independently on the northern route.

From Noto north-westwards as far as the centre of the island lay high ground known as the Hyblaean Plateau. Much importance had been attached to this high ground by Intelligence summaries. Possession of it was considered to be of the greatest strategical importance if military control was to be maintained over the south-east of the island. It was anticipated that the defence of the low coastal areas would be left to the Italian coastal defence divisions, and that the Italian field divisions would make a stand on the plateau. So far this had proved correct and only coastal troops had been met. In striking inland in the wake of Harpoon Force, therefore, we were likely to meet either the Livorno or Napoli Division—or possibly the Germans.

Noto stands at a height of about 500 feet, but the road rises steeply, and soon the column was on the top of hills at heights between 1,500 and 2,000 feet. The highest point reached on the first day was the trig point east of Palazzolo, a height of about 2,500 feet, which the Dorsets occupied for the night.

The road to Noto had possessed a reasonably hard surface, but this road was soft and powdery and blew in choking clouds of dust. Tanks and carriers became invisible in the dust screen that they threw up. The visibility of anyone passing these vehicles was about three yards, and drivers had to take their fortune and hope that nothing was coming the other way. Hair and moustaches turned white and the face became covered with a paste composed of dust and sweat. Altogether, it was a very uncomfortable journey.

The part that the Devons had to play with Harpoon Force was that of lorried infantry, but they had only one truck per company. Lieut.-Colonel Valentine decided to pool all his transport in an effort to keep one company up with the tanks. The remainder of the battalion had to start marching. Later, as more transport became available, a ferry system was established. The system was to keep picking the troops up from the rear and placing them at the front. Once placed at the front you had to keep on marching until you fell into last place again and it was your turn to be picked up. Writing of the difficulties that the

Devons experienced at that time, Lieut.-Colonel Valentine states: " That day we learnt a lot about ferrying troops in M.T. We used every form of transport we had. The anti-tank platoon portees did noble work and their drivers deserve special mention for their untiring work. The designer of the portee would probably have had a shock if he had seen them carrying complete platoons with all their arms and equipment. This they did frequently—often towing guns as well. Both Bren and mortar carriers carried as many as ten men. Lorries captured later in the day proved a god-send."

The Devons were not alone in their transport difficulties. The rest of the Brigade Group was also struggling on and making remarkably good speed. Some day, no doubt, there will be a victory parade and the troops will march past in threes—and the public will get the impression that that was how we used to advance. But what a shock they would get if we reproduced the real thing: marching troops; men riding on guns and carriers; men lorried on our own vehicles; men on captured Italian vehicles; men on motor-cycles and motor-cycle combinations; men on Italian motor tricycles; men on thoroughbred horses; men on mules; and even the donkey and cart! That was our motley cavalcade to Vizzini—but we got there.

Until the Devons approached Palazzolo the only signs of the enemy were abandoned and burnt-out lorries, guns and equipment. In the few villages that the troops passed through before Palazzolo the civilians appeared genuinely pleased to see them. They lined the streets and clapped their hands and asked for " cigarette " and " mangiare " (food). It was astonishing to see how quickly the children substituted the V sign for the Fascist salute.

Near Palazzolo the leading tanks were held up by anti-tank guns to the south of the town, and the assistance of the Devons was called for. " A " Company advanced to a commanding position to the left of the road together with a platoon of Vickers guns. As soon as the Brens and the heavy machine guns opened up, the enemy withdrew. Having completed this task, Major Hastings moved his company across the road to secure a ridge overlooking the town. In making this move they captured about 20 prisoners, one of whom was identified by Lieut. Beresford, the Brigade photographic interpreter, who was acting as liaison officer, as a member of the Napoli Division. We had met the Italian field division at last.

This hold-up had given the rest of the Devon battalion a chance to catch up with the armoured brigade and they were able to pass through Palazzolo together—but not until the infantry had assisted in clearing away obstructions caused by demolished buildings. Then the advance continued beyond the town and towards Vizzini.

Palazzolo was our first experience of a town which had been bombed by our own aircraft. The bombing had been very thorough. The place was a shambles and stank of dead bodies buried beneath the debris. It looked far worse than many of the towns which had been bombed in Malta, for the Sicilian houses showed the damage far more than the sturdy stone-built Maltese houses.

The Brigade Commander now came up to make a reconnaissance of positions for the night. The Devons obviously would guard the approaches beyond the town. The Dorsets were placed on the commanding feature south-east of the town, and the Hampshires on a lower but equally prominent feature to the west of the town. By this means all approaches by road to Palazzolo were blocked. In making the reconnaissance of the Dorset positions the Brigade Commander had to leave the main axis of advance and proceed up an unexplored path. He ordered the Intelligence Officer and his wireless operator to have their weapons at the ready. The precautionary measure proved to be necessary, because after a time they came to the top of a hill where there was a natural amphitheatre carved out of the rock. This place was filled with civilians and among them were three soldiers—all from the Napoli Division. We commanded them to surrender and two did so, but the third merged into the background and eventually disappeared in a hole in the rock at a place which might be described as the " grand circle." Rather nervously and covered by the guns of the others, the Intelligence Officer followed and on reaching the hole growled menacingly, hoping the while that it would be the Italian who would come out and not a hand grenade. The Italian did come out and with him an extremely pretty girl. It was obvious that they were young lovers and a long and tearful parting took place. Eventually the prisoners were handed over to someone else and the episode ended, leaving the girl in great distress at the loss of her Latin lover and the captors feeling uncomfortably Prussian.

We were rather proud of our exploit of capturing three prisoners, but the event became insignificant when about half an hour later about 200 of the Napoli were found congregated in the centre of the town waiting to give themselves up. Among them were a few members of the Livorno Division. We had known that an invasion of Malta had been planned to take place in the summer of 1942 and that it had been postponed when Rommel captured Tobruk. What we did not know until we interrogated these prisoners was that this division—the Livorno—had been selected to do the job. They were petrified with fear when they heard the news and were very pleased when the invasion was cancelled. It is a pity that this invasion did not take place, for had the Livorno come to Malta the defending troops would have had a field day and their morale would have risen to unprecedented heights.

That evening, shortly after Brigade Headquarters had settled in a position in rear of the Dorsets, news was received that a troop of medium guns had been shot up by Tiger tanks somewhere between Buscemi and Buccheri. To meet this menace to our flank the Brigade Commander ordered a patrol of the Hampshires with carriers to patrol that part of the road throughout the night. This news of Tiger Mark VI tanks caused rather a stir in high quarters—but afterwards the tanks turned out to be 75-mm. guns on self-propelled mountings.

Next day Harpoon Force moved on, followed by the Devons and the rest of the Brigade Group. There was nothing eventful about this move until we all piled up in front of Vizzini—but that is a story in itself and will be told later.

It is convenient at this time to consider the work being done by our supply services. The 346/231 Brigade Company, R.A.S.C., and Capt. P. J. Hurman, the Brigade R.A.S.C. Officer, were responsible for looking after us in this respect. An R.A.S.C. company normally contains a major, six captains and three subalterns, and has the use of ninety 3-ton load carriers. Its main task is to collect supplies from a field maintenance centre which has been established by Corps. From this point all commodities are drawn in bulk and transported to a supply point, selected by the Brigade R.A.S.C. Officer, where bulk is broken and where the units' vehicles collect supplies as required. It is laid down in theory that the distance from the field maintenance centre to the supply point should not be greater than forty miles, and that the distance from the supply point to the brigade area should not exceed twenty miles.

For combined operations, however, different arrangements have to be made, especially in the early stages. It was not possible to have so many supply vehicles landed in the first flights, and to counteract this difficulty each man was given a ration in a sealed tin which had to keep him going for the next two days. Unit vehicles carried a supply of composite rations, sufficient to feed the men for a further two days. After that it was assumed that the R.A.S.C. organization would function in the usual manner. The R.A.S.C. vehicles which did land with the assault carried ammunition only.

For the first twelve days of the Sicilian campaign 346/231 Brigade Company had only twenty-three vehicles instead of the usual ninety, and even then Corps produced only a further twelve 3-tonners. Instead of the R.A.S.C. being represented by eleven officers there were only Capt. P. J. Hurman and Capt. Baker and one other officer of 346 Company. The field maintenance centre did not become established until six days after the landing, and during this period all supplies had to be drawn from the beaches. When Brigade Group was at Palazzolo the beach was approximately forty miles distant, and later, at Vizzini, was sixty miles distant. It will be seen, therefore, that at this stage the lines of supply were stretched to the limit and that our R.A.S.C. company had insufficient vehicles and were extremely short of officers. Nevertheless, at this time and throughout the whole of the Sicilian campaign the Brigade was never once let down by the R.A.S.C. Never did a soldier have to go without a meal; never was there a shortage of petrol or ammunition.

How was it done? The answer is hard work and skilful planning of the officers concerned. The drivers of our limited numbers of vehicles kept up a constant ferry service of supplies, their task wherever possible being simplified by the intelligent planning of Capt. Baker.

Corps were also experiencing similar difficulties, and Capt. Hurman realized that as soon as we became static he might well have all his transport vehicles taken away from him. This, in fact, did happen when the Brigade reached Vizzini, but Capt. Hurman was ready for it. He had established a dump about four miles beyond Palazzolo, where ninety complete loads were laid on the ground, and from this dump the units drew, using their own vehicles. In establishing this dump, Capt. Hurman took a very great risk, for had the Brigade been forced to withdraw at this stage all these supplies on the ground would have been lost owing to lack of transport to remove them.

The only thing that favoured the R.A.S.C. at this time was that the water in Sicily was found to be more plentiful than had been anticipated. In the desert the transportation of water used to take up one-third of the space of all R.A.S.C. vehicles. The principal difficulty throughout the Sicilian campaign was the carriage of 25-pounder ammunition. Many formidable barrages were fired by the 165 Field Regiment, and in the general shortage of transport and the rapid moves which they had to make they were unable to keep up their supplies. Frequently, therefore, the R.A.S.C. transport had to carry as much as twenty to thirty loads of 25-pounder ammunition direct from the beach or field maintenance centre to the guns, and this entailed a journey which often exceeded eighty miles. Capt. Hurman, Capt. Baker and all the drivers of the 346/231 Brigade Company, R.A.S.C., who worked so hard to keep the Brigade supplied are to be congratulated on their efforts throughout the whole of the Sicilian campaign.

CHAPTER VI

VIZZINI

NO ONE IN THE BRIGADE GROUP would rank the battle for Vizzini as a victory. Each battalion attacked in turn and all met with reverses. Vizzini provides a three-day story of false confidence, bad intelligence, and of nibbling attacks when a large bite was required. It is a story, nevertheless, which is full of heroism and it contains some of the most amusing and interesting incidents of the whole campaign.

On the morning of 13th July the Brigade Group continued its advance, led by the Devons, who were following hard on the heels of Harpoon Force. It was at about 1000 hrs. when the Brigade Commander reached a point about three miles east of the town of Vizzini, and he was surprised to find that the area was under shell and mortar fire and our forces were at a standstill. On reaching the headquarters of Brigadier Richards he was informed that contact had been made with the enemy, who were probably Germans, and that the ground in front was unsuitable for tank warfare, and that it looked like a job for the infantry. At first sight it appeared ludicrous that such a strong force as Harpoon Force, which contained a brigade of tanks and supporting artillery, should be held up in this way, but Brigadier Richards pointed out that the ground fell away precipitously on both sides, making deployment impossible, and that the only possible approach to the town was along the road, which was very exposed to the commanding heights held by the enemy on the north-west of the town.

Lieut.-Colonel Valentine had made a thorough reconnaissance of the position, and he reported that the enemy strong-

VIZZINI.

[Crown Copyright Reserved

hold could only be reached after an approach over difficult open ground and that in his opinion it was a case for a night attack with artillery support. The Brigade Commander supported this view after he himself had gone forward to make a reconnaissance, and it was decided that a fresh battalion—the Hampshires—should make the attack that night.

Brigade Headquarters were established well forward in a very exposed position and the Hampshires were moved into an area between Brigade H.Q. and the Devons. For the rest of the morning and the early part of the afternoon all arrangements were made for the coming attack. By this time the Dorsets had moved up to a position in rear of Brigade H.Q.

About 1700 hrs. the Brigade Commander again visited the headquarters of Harpoon Force, and Brigadier Richards informed him that he had good reason to believe that the enemy had vacated their positions and that it was now possible to push on and take Vizzini. It is true that there had been a report from Tac. R. that movement of enemy M.T. had been seen leaving the Vizzini area, but otherwise there seemed to be no foundation for this report other than surmise. The intelligence proved to be entirely false and all our subsequent troubles at Vizzini dated from that moment.

The plan was now changed. The Hampshire attack was cancelled, and it was arranged that after the Devons had mopped up the Vizzini positions the Dorsets should take their place with Harpoon Force, and that the Brigade should then move on in the order Dorsets, Hampshires and Devons. The Brigade Commander then went to the headquarters of the Dorsets to inform Lieut.-Colonel Ray of this, but immediately on his return a message was received over the wireless from the Divisional Commander which necessitated yet another change of plan. Only one company of Dorsets was to move with Harpoon Force—the remainder of the Brigade to move independently on another road.

A conference was called to put the commanding officers of the Brigade Group in the picture, but before the conference could meet news was received that the advancing troops of the Devons were coming under heavy fire. The Brigade Commander then went forward to a point on the road known as Convent Hill and found that the scene there was one of confusion. Mortar shells were dropping all round, and tanks and M.T. were crowding the road in an attempt to make a speedy withdrawal. The leading tank and a scout car had been knocked out by anti-tank guns. From the wooded ground below Convent

Hill the Devons were exchanging machine-gun fire with the enemy in an attempt to cover their withdrawal.

Aftei the leading tank had been knocked out, Capt. H. V. Duke, of the Devons, had advanced with his company for another 600 yards. After going forward still farther to make a reconnaissance, he decided to withdraw his company, which he did with great skill. In the general confusion, Lieut. J. D. Campbell found himself and one of his sections behind the enemy positions and isolated from the rest of his company. They determined to carve a way back—and they were so successful that they silenced two enemy machine-gun posts *en route.* An amusing story is told of Lieut.-Colonel Valentine. The Colonel wished to speak to a tank commander whose head and shoulders were appearing from the top of a tank. The Colonel could not attract his attention in all the din, and finally in desperation he picked up a large stone and hurled it at the tank officer. It hit the tank with a clatter, whereupon the tank commander, thinking that his tank had been hit by a shell, rapidly disappeared, closing the hatch after him. Thus all further attempts at conversation became impossible, much to the disgust of Lieut.-Colonel Valentine. Apart from these incidents, there was nothing else amusing about this abortive attack. It cost the Devons 1 officer and 9 other ranks killed and 18 other ranks wounded.

The Brigade Commander then determined that a properly prepared attack should be made, and as all arrangements had been made previously for an attack by the Hampshires this plan was revived. The Brigade Intelligence Officer was dispatched to the headquarters of the Highland Division to receive the consent of the Divisional Commander and to ask for further artillery support other than that already provided. Consent for the attack was given, but the C.R.A. was unable to give extra artillery support that night, as his guns had not registered over the targets, and an area shoot without previous registration might prove extremely dangerous to our own troops.

The attack of the Hampshires that night went in at 2330 hrs. and supporting artillery fired concentrations from zero plus 20 to zero plus 60 on positions where the enemy were supposed to be located. " A " Company of the Hampshires were selected for the task and conflicting reports were received throughout the night regarding their progress. First we were informed that they had captured their objective; then came the news that they had not captured the whole of their objective and that the enemy were counter-attacking and a withdrawal appeared necessary.

The prearranged defensive fire was "laid on" and under cover of this the Hampshires withdrew. Their losses in this small action were considerable, among those killed being Lieut. J. D. le Brecht, a very courageous young officer.

We had given our own names to the ground in the area. There was Convent Hill, which provided a start line for most of the attacks, and the features held by the enemy were known as Scraggy Top Hill, Green Knoll and Single Hut Hill. There was also a fourth feature held by the enemy; but this was quite unknown to us until much later. In fact, one of the main advantages of the enemy at Vizzini was that the ground made location of his position extremely difficult.

For a clear picture of the fighting for Green Knoll and the difficulties with which our troops had to contend we are indebted to two excellent descriptive pieces of writing submitted by Sergt. H. W. Bowers and Pte. W. B. Collins, of the Hampshires. Both watched the artillery concentrations from the start line, and the Sergeant remarked to his platoon officer, Lieut. C. V. Williamson, that the shells were falling well to the right of their objective. Both writers also comment on the difficult ground over which they made their approach march. Sergt. Bowers says: "It was an evil piece of country, shrubs, small trees and huge boulders—men would step on to a boulder and then disappear in a huge pit or crevice. Before long I found it impossible to keep the platoon together." Sergt. Bowers found himself with a section commanded by Cpl. Byng and entirely separated from the rest of the platoon. This section went on alone and eventually captured an enemy post after some very close fighting with tommy-guns and grenades. One enemy position was found to be empty, and, not satisfied with this, Sergt. Bowers and Cpl. Byng went on to make a reconnaissance. Suddenly two German heads appeared over a wall and rifles fired at point-blank range. The shots missed and an Italian red grenade thrown by the Sergeant killed one of the Germans and seriously wounded another. They then found two other Germans pretending to be dead. The pretence was soon turned to reality. Then followed a running fight in a grotto which resulted in the capture of a German prisoner. About this time the Sergeant made contact with his platoon commander and it became obvious that there were many Germans in the area and that a counter-attack would not be long delayed. They were trying to lure men on with shouts of "Over here, 'A' Company," and "This way, 8 Platoon." Soon the Germans came on. They could be seen advancing in an orderly line up the hill, and under cover of all the fire-power they could raise the Hampshire platoon withdrew. At the bottom of the hill contact was made with the company commander, Major King, and it was at this point that Lieut. le Brecht made the attack with his platoon which resulted in the loss of his life.

The Hampshires sustained severe casualties, but their attack was not entirely without result. It was now realized that the Germans were holding not one position but about four, sited in depth, and each perfectly placed to give covering fire for the others. It rather resembled the three or four hill positions so frequently found in sand-table exercises. Furthermore, Sergt. Bowers had so frightened the prisoner that when he arrived back at Brigade Headquarters he gave full details of his unit and their arms. The position was therefore clear at last. We were confronted by the Reconnaissance Battalion of the Herman Goering Armoured Division. They were in strong positions; they were strong in automatic weapons; they were mobile; they had the support of armoured cars, anti-tank guns, heavy mortars and close-support infantry guns. To sum up, this was too tough a nut for a single company of infantry to crack. At the very least it was a task for a whole battalion with another battalion following up to consolidate the ground gained.

One amusing incident arose out of the Hampshire attack. Two Hampshire men got completely lost in the dark and eventually found themselves in the town of Vizzini. Here they found 1 officer and 45 other Italian soldiers, who immediately surrendered and were escorted back to camp next day. It illustrates the morale of the Italian forces in Sicily that, while their allies were putting up such a spirited fight on the heights above the town, yet down in the town itself such a large body of men should surrender so ignominiously.

On the morning of the 14th an attempt was made to frighten the enemy out of his positions by a display of force. It was a Divisional plan. There were to be concentrations of artillery fire. 153 Brigade and a battalion of United States troops were to approach Vizzini from the south while 152 Brigade approached from the north. Harpoon Force were to show themselves on the east and also on the east we were to make a diversion by an attack by one company, but strict instructions were received that this attack had not to be pressed home if stiff opposition was encountered.

It was perhaps unfortunate that the Dorsets were ordered to create the diversion, for by temperament the Dorsets are quite unsuited for that kind of thing. With them it is neck or nothing, and it was quite obvious to those in the know that Capt. Chilton and " B " Company would go through hell itself before they acknowledged that they were meeting stiff opposition.

However, " B " Company of the Dorsets made the attack and they captured the same objectives that the Hampshires had reached, which was a very creditable effort in the day time. The enemy, however, were not a bit impressed by the show of Divisional force and awarded us a hot reception. An officer and several men were killed and others wounded, and " B " Company were forced to withdraw. Sergt. A. Skingsley distinguished himself in this action. It was his platoon officer who had been killed and he undertook the difficult task of withdrawing the platoon under heavy fire. He was severely wounded and, though he was in great pain, he continued to conduct a fighting withdrawal. Finally he collapsed, but he insisted on being left with a tommy-gun, as he did not want to be a burden to the rest of the platoon. It was not until next day that a search party found him and brought him back.

After this third setback General Wimberley, commanding the Highland Division, determined that he would be held up no longer. He summoned his order group to the highest point in the area—3,000-foot Mount Lauro to the west of Buccheri. From here it was possible to see for about twenty miles in a northwesterly direction. The hills that we had been fighting for in front of Vizzini looked insignificant: Vizzini, a toy town resting in a valley, and behind the town Mount Altore, the only other mountain worthy of the name, which the General insisted on calling " Ben Lomond."

This time there was to be no mere display of force. The whole strength of the Highland Division and 231 Brigade was to be matched against the Germans on the ridge. All the Divisional guns, the guns of Harpoon Force and our own 165 Field Regiment were to hammer the enemy positions prior to 154 Brigade capturing them. Then the Dorsets were to follow up and take over the ground that 154 Brigade had captured, so that 154 might go on still farther and sweep the enemy from any reserve positions which he might be holding. 153 Brigade were ordered to capture the town of Vizzini and then push on with two battalions in the direction of Caltagirone.

It is impossible not to admire the enemy's defence at Vizzini. They must have known that they were outnumbered and they must have been very tired, for they had been rushed from Gela, where they had been fighting the Americans, to hold the threatened place in the line. Their stubborn defence of Vizzini probably lengthened the Sicilian campaign by a week or ten days, for had the Highland Division maintained the speed of their progress of the past three days there would have been no enemy defensive line running from Leonforte to Regalbuto, and then their defences on the Plain of Catania would have been quickly outflanked and rolled up. It is fortunate that we have a picture of what was happening behind the enemy's line. Pte. Barnes, of the Hampshires, was captured by an enemy fighting patrol. In his opinion, the enemy were nervous and jumpy. They did not interrogate him properly, only asking his nationality. They did not seem to know what to do with him, but kept marching him up and down a road. Eventually he was joined by other prisoners from the Hampshires and three Americans from the 45th Division, and they were all put down a disused well. While in the well they were given neither food nor drink. "That night," says Pte. Barnes, "a terrific barrage started and we all crouched in the bottom of the well for safety." Although the well was damp and stank abominably, several times during that barrage the Germans also jumped into the well for cover, one of them trembling like a leaf.

The barrage which Pte. Barnes was on the receiving end of was that planned by General Wimberley on Mount Lauro. The attack which it preceded commenced at 0100 hrs. on 15th July and was entirely successful. The enemy must have sensed that this time he was really up against it, for when our forward troops reached the crests of those familiar hills the Germans had vanished.

CHAPTER VII

QUEEN OF THE HILLS

THE 15TH JULY, which was spent at Vizzini, was a day of rest for most of us. At 0930 hrs. the Brigade Commander held a conference and announced that the Highland Division were now going to place us in reserve, and that our only duty was to provide a mobile column to patrol from Vizzini to Francofonte, thence to Scordia and eventually home via Militello.

The Hampshires were selected to provide this mobile column and it consisted of "C" and "D" Companies, a section of carriers, 3-inch mortars and machine guns, with a skeleton

Battalion H.Q., all mounted in transport. Lieut.-Colonel Spencer personally commanded the column, and apart from his own troops he had the assistance of a platoon of 4.2-inch mortars, a troop of 6-pounder anti-tank guns and a detachment of Sappers. The force was called " Shelleili Force " after the name of the Hampshires' H.Q. in Malta. The force was away for about two days and only once came in contact with the enemy. Enemy mortar and artillery fire caused them to deploy and a night was spent on the defensive. At first light the enemy were seen to have withdrawn and the column proceeded on its journey. There does not seem to have been very much point in providing a mobile column in the Scordia area, as two brigades of the Highland Division and a force of Sherman tanks were operating in the vicinity. It did, however, prove useful as an exercise, and valuable experience was gained which assisted the many similar columns which we produced later. When we assumed the independent role and reconnaissance could no longer be done for us by a Divisional reconnaissance unit, a Brigade reconnaissance unit on the " Shelleili " pattern was always used.

At 2100 hrs. on the 15th instructions were received that we were to leave the Highland Division and once again revert to the independent role under the command of XXX Corps. Our task for the following day was to follow up the Canadians and take over from them at Caltagirone, " The Queen of the Hills," and thus allow them sufficient freedom of movement to move forward to Enna.

We were sorry to leave the Highland Division, for our association with them had been a happy one. Because Brigadier Urquhart had been their G.S.O.1 in the desert and knew their methods, there was a complete absence of that shaking-down process which always took place when we came under command of other divisions. During the time we had been under command of the Highland Division, General Wimberley had his brigades fanning out all over the place. Each night at about 2100 hrs. he would hold a conference, which his Chiefs of Staffs, his Brigadiers and representatives of their staffs would attend, and the whole thing was sorted out. In the failing light to an audience covered with dust and the grime accumulated throughout the day, General Wimberley would explain what was happening, starting off with a short summary of the Sicilian battle as a whole, then giving dispositions of his own brigades and outlining the plan for the following day. Despite the fact that General Wimberley could not cope with names of Italian towns and called Caltagirone by a different name every time, it was an excellent system, especially from the intelligence point of view. By this method one knew exactly what had happened and what was going to happen, and it contrasted sharply with the methods of other divisions, who sent out written intelligence summaries which, when received, were sometimes out of date.

We learnt many other things from the Highland Division and especially of the use of wireless in a moving battle. The Highland Division renounced paper, but the Sicilian air resounded with soft Gaelic voices. To understand what was going on one had to know the name or nickname of everyone in that Division, and although security experts raised their eyebrows at expressions such as " Roy's Boys," the name given to us, the whole procedure was justified by the fact that it worked.

Early next morning the Brigade moved on to Caltagirone, the order of march being 1 Dorsets, 2 Devons, 1 Hamps and Bde. H.Q. The route chosen was through Mineo, the reason being that the direct route was crowded out by Canadians. Little of interest happened on this march except that a German Mark VI Tiger tank was seen burnt out on the side of the road. Throughout the Sicilian campaign every tank reported was a Mark VI and every gun an 88-mm., but here was visible proof that the Germans really did have some of their latest tanks in Sicily. The Brigade Commander and the reconnaissance parties from battalions took the direct road to Caltagirone, passing through the town of Grammichele.

One of the most surprising things about the Sicilian campaign up to this time was that we had not met any obstructions such as demolished bridges, mines and booby traps. The result was that whenever we moved we were able to advance about twenty miles a day. It was not until we reached Caltagirone that we came up against the work of the German engineers in rather a dramatic fashion. A bridge on the road leading out of Caltagirone had been demolished and this took the Canadian Sappers some time to repair, causing considerable congestion in the town itself. At the foot of the hill beyond Caltagirone the Brigade Commander left the main axis of advance and traversed the secondary road three or four times in an effort to find suitable defensive positions for the Devons and the Dorsets. A few minutes after he had passed over a certain stretch of the road in his jeep, which also carried the Brigade I.O. and a wireless operator, a horse and cart came along carrying four Sicilian adults and a child. Suddenly there was a tremendous explosion and the whole contraption was flung into the air and all that remained of the horse and the five human beings were bloody bits of " butcher's meat " scattered over the road and adjoining fields. Later from the same spot the Canadian Sappers lifted half a dozen German Teller anti-tank mines. The incident made us think not a little.

Caltagirone, " Queen of the Hills," had been heavily bombed by American planes and had lost most of the dignity usually associated with royalty. The inhabitants had fled to the hills, but about the time we arrived their hunger was driving them back to the town again. They complained that the retreating Germans had treated them very badly, raping their women and stealing all their food. It was a story we were to hear over and over again as we journeyed through Sicily. Most of the civilians detested the Germans and were only too glad to give information regarding their movements. It was at Caltagirone that we first started the technique of having a linguist well forward with our advancing troops to pick up any information of the enemy which the civilians were willing to supply. Caltagirone had been badly looted, firstly by the retreating Germans and secondly by the more undesirable types among the civilians who had remained behind when the others had fled.

On the evening of 16th July patrols of the 1st Dorsets and 2nd Devons were ordered to move northwards and then to the east towards Piazza Armerina, where the Canadians were reported to be held up. About midnight the patrol of the Dorsets reported that they were held up on the road to Raodusa by mines, and that one of their carriers had been blown up and casualties sustained. Early next morning the same patrol reported that they were held up by a demolished bridge and that bridging equipment would be required immediately if they were to make further progress. There was only one road, and the Devon patrols were also using this. The result was that they piled up on top of the Dorsets and it became obvious that if we were to reach Piazza Armerina in time to affect the battle some other route must be found. The direct route and the road via Mirabella were explored by the Brigade Commander. He was probably the first man to enter Mirabella, and the inhabitants turned out in force to give a reception. Beyond Mirabella, however, another bridge was found to be demolished, and the direct road was no better because the Germans had demolished a bridge there also after permitting one of the Canadian brigades to get beyond it. It was obvious now that we could not get to Piazza Armerina without getting hopelessly involved with the Canadian troops who were already overcrowding the roads.

The Brigade Commander therefore sought permission to act in an independent role along the road to Raddusa, and the Corps Commander agreed. Our troops who had already started in the direction of Piazza Armerina were hurriedly recalled and every effort was made to repair the demolition on the Raddusa road. Thus began our fighting advance which took us over forty miles due north to Agira, then a further ten miles east to Regalbuto.

The demolished bridge on the Raodusa road did not provide the serious obstacle that was at first anticipated, and Major Courtie and the men of 66 Field Company, R.E., quickly made a diversion which crossed the dry bed of the river. A most unfortunate accident occurred at this demolition. The balustrade of the bridge collapsed and buried in its debris some of the men who were working in the bed of the river below. Five of the Sappers became casualties in this incident. During the rest of the day the Dorset patrol made good progress, and it was not until 1900 hrs. that evening that a report was received that contact had been made with the enemy, who were holding the line of the river about two miles south of the town. That day we had made an advance of over twenty miles.

At 2100 hrs. the Brigade Commander called a conference of his order group at the point where the road makes a T junction approximately four miles south of Raodusa. As he reached the appointed place in his jeep an ominous whirring sound was heard in the air and four mortar bombs were dropped about 100 yards to the left. The jeep was quickly backed about 200 yards down the road, where the commanding officers of the other units had assembled. Most of that conference was spent in a ditch, as " stonk " after " stonk " of mortar bombs descended round us, several direct hits being obtained on the T junction itself. The Brigade Commander was not satisfied with the description of the forward troops as given by the commanding officers and he determined to have a look for himself, to the horror of the I.O. and wireless operator, who realized that this entailed a journey past the T junction and then along a skyline in open country. Fortunately it turned out that the mortar fire had been put down by the enemy to cover their withdrawal and nothing disastrous occurred.

That night battalions were settled in defensive positions with the Devons and Dorsets to the west and east of the road respectively and the Hampshires in reserve in the area of Mount Crunici. There was no enemy activity during the night, but a patrol reported that the bridge of the River Gornalunga had been demolished. The following morning, with the assistance of our Sappers, who had made a diversion across the dry bed of the river, the mobile column of the Hampshires entered the town of Raodusa without opposition. The rest of the Brigade Group followed and as we passed through the town we noticed that the Dorsets had painted up on prominent walls their " 63 " sign and also the sign of the Maltese Cross. We had been rather amused at the insistence of the Brigade Commander in having signs placed the whole way along our axis of advance, but our experience with the Highland Division (the " Highway Decorators ") had shown us the value of these signs, and by the time we had finished the Sicilian campaign we were the best-signed formation in the island.

That day, 18th July, we did not make much more than an advance of seven miles and at midday the mobile column of the Dorsets reported that they had made contact with the enemy and were under heavy mortar fire. We had reached the positions from which the Hampshires were later to fight the battle for the River Dittaino.

That day Brigade Headquarters selected their most uncomfortable position, on the top of a hill and close to a jagged sulphurous outcrop of rock. The ground was covered with rank weeds: there was no protection from the sun, and the heat during the afternoon was almost unbearable.

CHAPTER VIII

THE CROSSING OF THE RIVER DITTAINO

IT WAS ABOUT 1600 HRS. on the afternoon of 18th July when the Brigade Commander went forward with the Brigade I.O. to visit the forward positions of " A " Company of the 1st Dorsets on the hill called Destrigtilla, which lies to the east of the road which was the axis of advance of the Brigade.

It was a very hot afternoon and the positions of the company, pointed out by Major Knapp, were very exposed and devoid of all cover from the sun. On top of the hill was also sited an O.P. of the 165 Field Regiment. This part of the countryside was the most unattractive met by the Brigade so far on the island. The landscape consisted of a series of ridges at right angles to the line of advance, with heights varying from about 800 to 2,000 feet. The most prominent feature was Mount Judica, rising to 2,500 feet about five miles to the east, which was too far away to affect the tactical position as far as our battle was concerned. Every field contained either short, dry stubble or rank weeds and prickles. Everything which grew on the ground seemed to contain a thorn or a barb of some description—and they found their way inside clothing, causing much discomfort.

Earlier in the day their positions had come under heavy mortar fire, but all was peaceful as the Brigade Commander made his reconnaissance. Ahead the ground sloped away to the valley which contained the River Dittaino, but it was not possible to see right down into the valley owing to intervening hills. Beyond the valley the ground rose sharply again to heights of over 1,000 feet. The valley itself was apparently level for about a thousand yards and appeared to offer little cover. It was known that the road crossed the river by an iron bridge which had not been blown by the enemy. The problem therefore was to secure this bridge intact and capture the commanding feature to the north of it. The answer appeared to be a surprise attack by night.

At 1730 hrs. the Brigade Commander held a conference. As we had fallen into the habit of battalions taking on opposition by rotation, and as it was now the turn of the Hampshires, Lieut.-Colonel Spencer was ordered to capture the river crossing and the position astride the road to the north. The Dorsets and the Devons were ordered to follow up and take up positions on the high ground south of the river to the east and west of the road respectively. The Devons were also told to hold in readiness a mobile column to exploit the success of the Hampshires. The column was to consist of a company of infantry, two sections of carriers, an anti-tank troop, an F.O.O., and a strong reconnaissance party of R.E. At this time the Hampshires were in reserve and concentrated in the area of the town of Raodusa.

After the conference the Brigade Commander went forward to make another reconnaissance with Colonel Spencer. As a result of this reconnaissance the C.O. of the Hampshires formulated the following plan, the essence of which was simplicity. The first objectives were the two hills on the near side of the valley called Cugno and Hill 370. These were to be captured by " C " Company and " B " Company respectively. Then " A " Company and " D " Company were to pass through and capture the high ground beyond the valley known as Bufali on the right of the road and a large nameless ridge to the left of the road. Then both companies were to exploit to a general east—

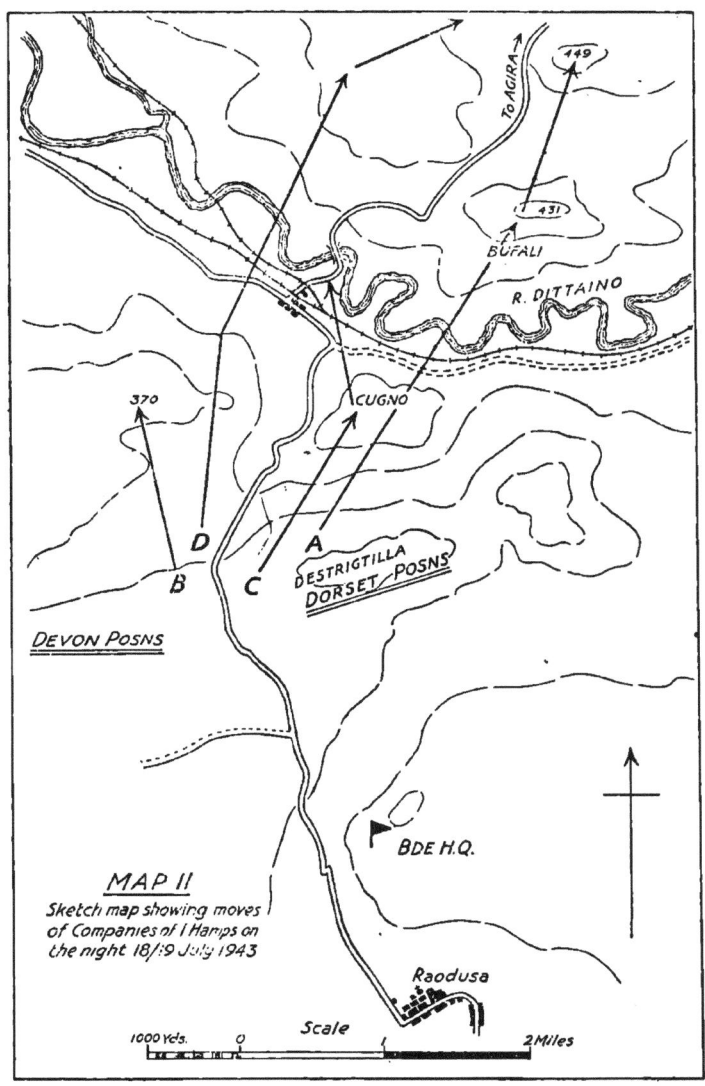

west line astride the road through point 449. The timings were as follows: "C" and "B" Companies to cross the start line at 2330 hrs. and "A" and "D" Companies to pass through objectives of leading companies at 0045 hrs.

As the attack was to be a silent one, the artillery plan was arranged so that fire was available as and when required. Four tasks, all of them concentrations or area shoots in the Bufali area, were arranged with 165 Field Regiment.

After "A" and "D" Companies had passed through, "C" Company was to advance to the bridge and cover the immediate approaches. "B" Company was to be held as a reserve for further use by the battalion commander if required. One section of carriers was detailed to exploit up the road leading to Agira to a limit of three miles north of the river. A platoon of R.E. was placed under command to remove any mines or road blocks which might be found on the road axis.

In considering the action it is perhaps best to view it first in the light of the formal report submitted by the Hampshires and then to look at some of the individual feats of bravery and general skill of arms and manœuvre which led to success.

The report reads as follows:

" There was just sufficient light to allow platoon commanders to get a quick look at the ground. For the attack itself the moon was two days past full. The concentration of the battalion took place in M.T. and due to an error the transport was brought too far forward and drew sharp artillery fire from the enemy. The two forward companies moved to time and secured their objectives without opposition. By approx. 0200 hrs. the other two companies had crossed the river and the R.E. platoon with Tac. Battalion H.Q. had moved up to the railway station, which was a few hundred yards south of the bridge. By 0300 hrs. ' C ' Company was occupying the bridgehead north of the river and at this time both the forward companies were thoroughly engaged by enemy M.G. and mortar fire. R/T communication failed, but the C.O. received information from time to time from liaison N.C.Os. of the forward companies. As the enemy opposition was strong, artillery support was asked for on two of the preselected tasks, and both company commanders reported that this artillery fire was most effective in breaking up the defence. On the left ' D ' Company, using 2-inch mortars, grenades and firing L.M.Gs. and T.S.M.Gs. from the hip, made good progress in the dark. On the right ' A ' Company, owing to difficult and steep going, postponed their attack until the beginning of first light. On each enemy front the enemy's fire was ineffective due to our troops keeping close to the hillsides, so that mortar fire fell behind and below them and L.M.G. fire was generally over their heads. At first light both companies advanced with great speed under cover of their own weapons and 3-inch mortars brought up by carriers. In spite of the strength and depth of the position and the steep, rocky hillsides up which the troops had to move, the enemy put up small resistance and an hour later the leading companies reached the final objectives, having mopped up all opposition, and captured 20 officers and 864 other ranks for the loss of only a few wounded themselves."

Thus reads the official account, which in its precise modesty underestimates the importance of this action. The River Dittaino proved at that time of the year to be waterless, but nevertheless steep banks led down to the dry bed of the river, and had the bridge been blown it might well have proved a lengthy undertaking for the R.E. to provide a diversion. Any R.E. work in the area of the bridge would most certainly have been under fire from the commanding ridges to the north. Even with the bridge intact traffic passing that way for the next two or three days was shelled by German artillery from the east. Had this traffic been compelled to slow down at a difficult diversion it would have provided a wonderful target for these German guns; as it was they did little damage.

The enemy meant to hold this position. Clearly he was worried by our rapid advance northward and he must have been desperately anxious to organize his defences around Agira. Few Italians were encountered after the round-up of prisoners in this battle, and it appears as if the Germans had collected all available Italian soldiers and put them along the line of the River Dittaino, relying on the natural strength of the position rather than on the fighting quality of the troops.

In view of the fact that the Italians did fight, it was a great triumph for the two companies of the Hampshires to put to flight over a thousand soldiers in such strong positions, and great credit is due to the leadership of Major R. King, of " A " Company, and Capt. D. R. J. Edkins, who commanded " D " Company.

Major King was the first to cross the river with his company and then he led them against difficult objectives on a succession of steep heights. He carried out successfully the extremely difficult task of reorganizing his company in the darkness and under enemy mortar and machine-gun fire. At first light he attacked again and cut off the enemy in their reserve positions, and his company were responsible for killing many of the enemy and taking over 400 of them prisoner.

Capt. Edkins had similar difficulties to contend with, and these difficulties were increased by the short, dry stubble which made a silent approach impossible, and by fires caused by artillery fire which silhouetted our troops against the glare. At first light Capt. Edkins personally led the pursuit of the enemy and finally captured the heights which dominated the valley.

Great initiative was shown by both these officers. When the wireless link failed they were out of touch with the commanding officer and could no longer rely on his direction. The only means of communication was the slow and uncertain way of runner in the dark. More timid men would have hesitated, but they went on alone and it was here that the clarity and simplicity of Lieut.-Colonel Spencer's plan were to show their value.

Many acts of individual bravery took place in this battle and many more must have passed unnoticed in the dark. A typical example of the fighting prowess of the Hampshires is shown by the action of Cpl. C. Green. When his section was held up by an enemy fortified machine-gun position, he ordered his own section Bren gunner to give covering fire while he attacked with grenade and tommy-gun. All the enemy in the post were either captured or killed.

Only well-trained men could have fought this difficult action in the dark, and the thorough and systematic training of the Hampshires proved itself when it was needed. It is interesting to note that both forward companies of the battalion employed the same battle drill. On encountering an enemy position the leading platoon engaged by grenade and tommy-guns. While this close in-fighting was occupying all the enemy's attention the second platoon worked round to the flank or the rear and cut off the enemy's retreat. The third platoon was left in reserve to meet any contingency which might arise.

The men showed great skill not only with their own weapons but with captured enemy weapons which were found in great numbers. These were immediately turned round and put to our own use.

Lastly, the battle for the River Dittaino was a great test of physical strength and endurance. Here again hard training proved its worth because the men knew in advance the difficult ground which lay in front of them and they went forward with confidence in their own stamina.

An adequate but simple plan, fine leadership, discipline and

[Crown Copyright Reserved

FIGHTING MEN.
Brigadier K. P. Smith, O.B.E., takes the salute at the march past of the 1st Bn. The Hampshire Regiment in Malta,

training in battle drill and in weapons, physical fitness and confidence—these were the things which resulted in victory and which made the battle of the River Dittaino a perfect little set-piece of military manœuvre.

CHAPTER IX

" SOUTH OF AGIRA "

THE BATTLE FOR THE BEACHES AT MARZAMEMI had been a Brigade action. After that all our battles had seldom involved more than about two companies, while the rest of the Brigade were strung out farther down the road. From now onwards, however, the Brigade fought as a whole and at times had all its reserves committed.

It had been planned that the success of the Hampshires at the crossing of the River Dittaino should be followed up by a mobile column provided by the 2nd Devons, who were to continue the advance northwards and if possible capture Agira. The mobile column consisted of " B " Company under command of Capt. Spread, the Devon carriers and a troop of anti-tank guns. Unfortunately the column was delayed for nearly an hour at the river crossing by a lorry which had got stuck in the deviation, and this delay proved to have far-reaching effects on the action that was to take place later in the day. The Devons were still very short of transport and the column was fortunate in finding two four-seater Italian Spa lorries, which were quickly put in order and did good service for the rest of the campaign.

About seven miles south of Agira the Devon column had their first sight of the town. We had never seen anything quite like this before. Lieut. Peebles, our officer observer, described it as being like an illustration out of Grimm's Fairy Tales. Imagine a medieval town perched on the top of Scafell or Snowden and you get some idea of what it was like. The highest point was a rocky pinnacle, rising from the centre of the town, surmounted by a tower.

But what astonished the Devons even more than their first view of the town was that in full view the Germans were coming down over the foothills beneath the town and were moving into position on a ridge, known as Point 462, which lay to the right of the road. Through their glasses they could see the machine gunners putting their guns into position and sections disappearing as they got into slit trenches. An officer from 165 Field Regiment was up with the Devon column, but at this crucial moment his wireless refused to function and no artillery fire could be brought to bear. Thus this misfortune, coupled with the unavoidable delay at the start, allowed the enemy to prepare to meet our advance, whereas otherwise they might have sustained heavy losses.

It was obvious that the Devons must push on before the enemy became too firmly entrenched. Capt. Eteson and his carriers soon made contact and succeeded in shooting up some of the Germans who were doing some last-minute digging. Capt. Spread and his company, who were following up the carriers, came under machine-gun fire about 1,500 yards away from the main enemy position. He immediately debussed his company and, sending one platoon round to the right of the road, he moved the other two platoons round to the left of the road with the object of seizing a long rocky ridge which was known as Massa Scardelli. This ridge, running east and west, and about 1,000 yards long, was surmounted by grey rocks, among which the enemy could be clearly seen. Its eastern half dropped through orchards to the main road near a bridge which had been demolished. In the orchard stood a large red farmhouse and this was found to be occupied by the enemy. Machine-gun fire was coming from it and all along the rocky ridge above. With the support of the battalion mortars he led his company towards the objective. Lieut. Scott and Cpl. C. E. Butler distinguished themselves in this action. With great dash and determination they led No. 11 Platoon up the rocks and drove out the Germans from the crest. Lieut. Scott was killed whilst assisting a wounded man under heavy machine-gun fire. The other platoon, under Lieut. Pearson, captured the objective on the right of the ridge, where the ground was less difficult, while on the other side of the road the third platoon was almost level.

The Dorsets were following up the Devons very closely, and when the Devons were held up " A " and " C " Companies of the Dorsets came under accurate mortar fire and several casualties were sustained.

The Brigade Commander had been up with the forward troops all day and he was without the assistance of his Staff officers, as both the Brigade Major and Intelligence Officer had been delayed in leaving the last Brigade location, and had then been held up by enemy shell fire in the area of the bridge across the River Dittaino. By the time the Brigade H.Q. caught up

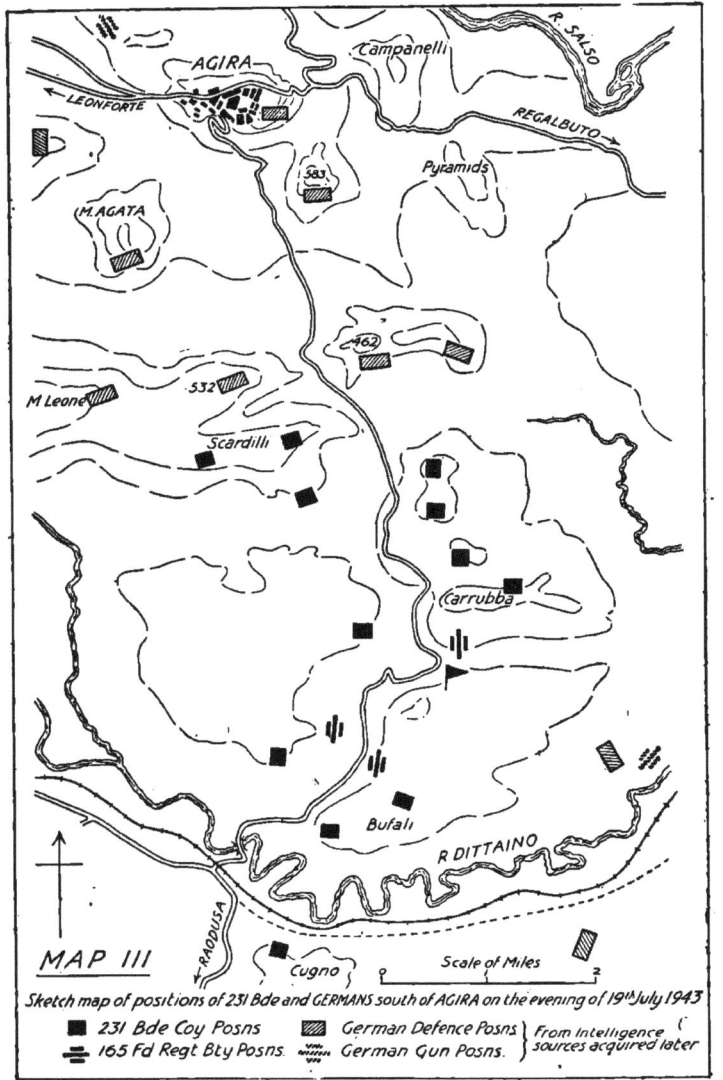

with the Brigade Commander, the position had been stabilized, and the Dorsets had taken over the area on the right of the road with " C " and " A " Companies forward and " B " and " D " Companies in the rear. Throughout the day the forward platoons had been under constant mortar and machine-gun fire and under cover of darkness Lieut.-Colonel Valentine sent forward " A " and " C " Companies to relieve " B " Company of the Devons, who came back for a well-earned rest.

The situation of the Brigade at this time was extremely insecure. We had advanced about ten miles beyond the rest of the Eighth Army. The Canadians were making slow progress somewhere behind us on our left, and there was a gap between us and the Highland Division on our right which was large enough for a Corps to pass through. The Brigade was strung out over a length of about five miles of road. The forward platoons of the Devons and Dorsets were facing what was obviously strong German opposition in defence of Agira. Enemy forces were known to be on our right flank also, and the remaining companies of the Dorsets and the Brigade Support Company were deployed to meet this threat. The left flank was wide open and we were least prepared to meet a threat from that direction. The Hampshires were allotted the task of guarding the tail. Our lines of supply ran from Raodusa across the bridge of the River Dittaino. This road was under shell fire from guns that appeared to be sited in the River Dittaino Valley about two miles to the east. A road approached the Hampshires' positions along the valley of the River Dittaino, both from the east and from the west, and an attack could easily come in either direction, and if such an attack had been successful in cutting our supply road we would have been isolated. There were very few places in the area suitable as sites for headquarters, and Brigade H.Q. was sited on a forward slope. There was a wonderful view of Agira and it occurred to some of us that the Germans in Agira would have a wonderful view of us. Two days later when the shells of a heavy artillery concentration fell all round, we were certain of it.

The 19th July was a black day for the Brigade Group. The Dorsets and the Devons came under heavy fire. The Hampshires, in an effort to stop the enemy shelling from the right flank, prepared the fighting patrol from which Capt. Guest and many other men of his company never returned. The anti-tank gunners lost a 17-pounder gun and sustained casualties. 165 Field Regiment were particularly unfortunate in losing Major R. H. Daubney and Capt. A. G. Dodd, of 64th Battery. Both these officers were killed when a mortar bomb made a direct hit on their scout car. In the early stages of the campaign our casualties had been very light; they were now on the increase, and by the end of the day, in killed, wounded and missing, the Brigade Group had lost 13 officers and 143 other ranks.

In nine days the Brigade had advanced a distance of approximately 140 miles and they had been fighting most of the way. It was the original intention earlier in the day to make a night attack against Agira, but the infantry were completely exhausted and the attack was postponed. There was no doubt about it that at this time we had the enemy on the run, and had such an attack been made we might have succeeded in doing in one night as much as it took the whole of the Canadian Division a week to accomplish. On the other hand, a night attack against the strong Agira position with exhausted men might well have ended in disaster. The Brigade Commander's decision to consolidate and remain in the positions that we had gained received the full approval of the Corps Commander.

On the morning of 20th July the Brigade Commander held a conference at which it was decided to continue the offensive by pushing the two forward battalions on to prominent features, approximately one kilometre nearer to Agira, while the Hampshires followed up the success by an attack against a hill known as Point 583 which lay right under the cliffs of Agira. The Brigade Commander made his reconnaissance, but before the plan could be put into operation news was received that we had come under command of the 1st Canadian Division, and that we were to make no further move until the Canadians had reached a position immediately west of Agira which they were expected to do the following night. Therefore, that day the two forward battalions remained in their rather insecure positions and came under extremely heavy shelling. Most of the main road was under direct observation from the summit of Agira, and, although single vehicles could move up and down, groups of vehicles always attracted attention and drew fire. The road leading to the forward Devon positions was especially exposed and their carriers did noble work taking forward ammunition, food and water, bringing back the wounded and keeping the 4.2-inch mortar of the Support Company supplied with bombs.

Both the Devons and the Dorsets sent out patrols. One Devon patrol, under Lieut. C. A. Osborne, confirmed that the enemy immediately to the front had not withdrawn. The Dorsets sent out a patrol from " A " Company commanded by Lieut. R. P. Royle, and another patrol from " B " Company commanded by

Lieut. Brown. "A" Company patrol came under heavy fire from the 462 feature and Lieut. Royle and several other men were wounded. Pte. Boundsall, a stretcher-bearer, put in some extremely heroic work in rescuing the men who were wounded in this patrol. Lieut. Brown's patrol did not come under fire, but he came back with the valuable information that the feature which he was reconnoitring and which was called the Council House, because of the appearance of the buildings on it, contained enemy who were thought to be Germans.

During the morning an armoured car was seen to leave Agira and come down the main road. No. 7 Platoon of "A" Company, 2nd Devons, waited for it and then opened up with two Bren guns. The car came to a stop, reversed rapidly up the road and then turned over into a ditch. The driver had been seriously wounded. He was extricated later by a patrol, but was found to be suffering from severe burns from which he shortly died. From this prisoner and from others it became possible to make an estimate of the forces that were opposing us. On the right of the road facing the Dorsets were four companies and the headquarter company of 34th Infantry Regiment of the Livorno Division. The Italians stated that they were holding the Agira positions in conjunction with the Herman Goering Division, but there appeared to be little co-ordination between the German and Italian forces. Facing the Devons were German troops belonging to the 29th Panzer Grenadier Regiment of the 15th Panzer Division. The armoured car which the Devons had knocked out belonged to the reconnaissance unit of this division. Later, German identifications were obtained from the Dorsets' front. These troops must have been sent in to fill the gaps when the Italians began to desert in large numbers. Little was known of the enemy forces which had ambushed the Hampshire patrol, but they were known to include German infantry with machine guns, supported by at least one 88-mm. gun and four tanks.

On the morning of 21st July the Brigade Major and the I.O. met Major-General Simmonds, Commander of the 1st Canadian Division, at his headquarters near Valquarnera. The General outlined his future plans as follows: the 3rd Canadian Brigade were to take over the area of the Dittaino Bridge from the Hampshires, thus enabling them to close up with the rest of the Brigade Group. Then the 3rd Canadian Brigade were to attack the enemy positions in the Dittaino Valley to the east which had given the Hampshires so much trouble. Meantime the other two Canadian brigades were to capture Leonforte and then Agira. After that we were to lead the Canadian advance towards Regalbuto.

As we were to remain static for the time being, patrolling continued. A Devon patrol under Sergt. Hiscox and Cpl. Gannon was dispatched to find out the situation on Point 532. They returned with the information that the hill was definitely occupied by the enemy, who appeared to be dug in in three platoon localities. The Dorsets continued their patrols against Point 462 and sustained further casualties. The Hampshires patrolled cautiously to the east in an attempt to gain more information about the cleverly concealed enemy positions.

During the day "A" Company of the 2nd Devons were heavily mortared and shelled and had about 20 casualties. Stretcher-bearers and carriers did excellent work in getting the wounded back under fire. The Dorsets' company positions came under intermittent shell and mortar fire which did little damage. Their main problem was the supply of ammunition, food and water to "C" Company, the most forward company, which could only be carried out during the hours of darkness.

At 1400 hrs. on 22nd July the Brigade Commander held a conference. The general situation at this time was as follows: the 1st and 2nd Canadian Brigades had captured Leonforte and were reorganizing. The Divisional Commander was anxious to keep the enemy on the run and decided to attack Agira that night. Our role was to threaten Agira from the south. With artillery support the Dorsets were ordered to attack Point 462 and the Devons Point 532. This meant an advance of approximately 1,000 yards for each battalion. The attack was timed for 2300 hrs. The Hampshires were to be ready with two mobile companies. If no enemy resistance was met they were to proceed up the main road to Agira. If enemy resistance was found to be strong, then they were ordered to work round the right flank, but not farther forward than Point 583.

We were still under heavy shelling and mortar fire, and the 165 Field Regiment and the 4.2-inch mortars of the Support Company replied whenever possible, but it was extremely difficult to locate the enemy weapons. Some were obviously 105-mm. and 150-mm. guns sited well behind Agira. The Devons complained that they were being mortared from the left flank, while the Hampshires' area and the artillery areas were troubled by guns and mortars firing from the right flank and somewhat in our rear. It was on this day that the area which contained Brigade H.Q., Battalion H.Q. of the 2nd Devons and a battery of 165 Field Regiment was heavily shelled. The only casualties were sustained by the Gunners, who lost one 25-pounder and had 1 sergeant killed and 7 other men wounded.

The night attack was preceded by an artillery barrage on the objectives, in which our own 165 Field Regiment was supported by the guns of 93 Medium Regiment, R.A., and 142 (Sp.) Regiment, R.A. The Devons' attack on Point 532 was put in by " C " Company on the right and " D " Company on the left. On the left the attack went well and after some sharp fighting " D " Company secured their objective. It was not so easy for " C " Company, who had advanced over the top of the hill and down the far side, but had bypassed some German machine guns which were shooting them up from the rear. They reported heavy casualties, especially among officers, Capt. G. Nock and Lieuts. Maloney and Lambert having become casualties. Lieut. Maloney had been rushing a machine-gun post with Pte. Drew when he was hit. Drew went on alone, but received a severe wound in the head from which he afterwards died.

While " C " and " D " Companies were making this attack, " B " Company and Battalion H.Q. were shelled continuously for two hours and sustained a number of casualties. The Second-in-Command, Major G. R. Young, and the Adjutant, Capt. T. A. Holdsworth, did excellent work standing by the wireless during this heavy shelling and keeping the Brigade Commander in touch with the situation.

Both Major Biggart and Capt. Duke, commanding the forward companies, asked for assistance in clearing up the position on Point 532. Lieut.-Colonel Valentine then ordered Capt. Spread to move " B " Company on to the right end of the feature 532, where the German machine guns were giving most trouble. Their advance was over most difficult country in the dark and ended with a steep climb of about 1,200 feet up a rocky slope. They arrived at the exact place required and this proved to be the turning point in the battle. When the Germans saw " B " Company working round their flank they hurriedly withdrew, leaving machine guns, machine pistols and equipment of all types.

Daylight revealed the Devons firmly in position on Point 532 and all the companies busy digging in. Once again the main difficulty was the supply of ammunition, food and water. Capt. Eteson reconnoitred in every direction but found that owing to the numerous deep wadis which surrounded the position, carriers could not possibly get up to the companies. Everything had to be man-handled—a long and tedious proceeding. " C " Company managed to get two very small donkeys. The commanding officer met a private leading one of the donkeys down the hill.

"Can he carry the rations?" inquired the C.O.

"Yes, sir," replied the temporary muleteer cheerfully, "but we 'as to carry the donkey."

Meantime, on the other side of the road the Dorsets were attacking Point 462. This was a three-company attack. The plan was that the attack should open with " B " Company leading on the right directed against the part of the feature known as the Council Houses. " D " Company were to follow them with the intention of passing through and securing the right-hand end of 462 Ridge. " C " Company took the left flank and were ordered to capture the left end of the ridge. " B " Company soon gained their objective, but as it was an extremely dark night without any moon, " C " and " D " Companies crossed each other's path with the result that they attacked each other's end of the ridge. Despite this confusion and that the ridge was found to be extremely steep and defended by Germans, the Dorsets' attack was completely successful. In this action Capt. A. C. W. Martin again distinguished himself. He attacked an enemy post by himself, shot two of the occupants with his revolver, and when the third shot failed to go off he picked up a rifle from the ground and disposed of another by using the butt, and he was eventually found at the bottom of a slit trench grappling with the fourth occupant. Fine leadership on the part of Lieut. Stoy played a large part in the success of this action.

As ordered, the Hampshires moved forward during the night and by the morning of 24th July they were disposed with two companies in front of Hill 462, one company behind Hill 462 and one company on the opposite side of the road in the vicinity of the Devons' Battalion H.Q.

At midday the Brigade Commander held a conference. He stated that the Canadians were going to make an attack on Agira late that evening, and that the Brigade Group was to co-operate by stopping all exits from Agira, especially on the east side. The burden of this fell on the Hampshires, who were ordered to occupy a feature known as Campanelli, which lay on the far side of the Agira—Regalbuto road.

The plan of the Hampshires to carry out the orders dictated by the Canadians was as follows:

" C " Company were to move forward to a twin-topped hill which we called the Pyramids. This company was to act as a secure base. " D " Company were to take up a position in front of the Pyramids but south of the main road. " A " Company were to gain positions astride the main road, while " B " Company were to push two platoons forward on to the Campanelli feature itself.

Zero hour was timed for 1800 hrs. and the Hampshires' move forward commenced at 2000 hrs., at which time they had no news of the Canadian situation. By 2 o'clock in the morning the Hampshires had taken up the positions according to plan, but news was received that the Canadians had not captured Agira but were proposing to make another attack immediately. The Hampshires therefore changed their plan, and " A " Company were moved from the position astride the main road, which was very exposed and completely overlooked from the heights of Agira, to the Campanelli feature, which offered a certain amount of cover in the way of shrub and undergrowth. Just before first light the Hampshires heard that the Canadian attack on Agira had failed and that, in fact, they were some six miles from the town on the west. The battalion was ordered to hold the Campanelli feature with two companies, but to lie low during the day time until such time as the Canadians could organize another attack.

Dawn showed these two forward companies of the Hampshires to be in a very difficult position. The Campanelli feature was almost too large to be held by two companies. Its disadvantages were that it was entirely overlooked by the dominating heights of Agira, and its western slopes were extremely steep and divided into sectors by high prickly-pear hedges. This made a good field of fire difficult, but, on the other hand, gave the enemy a covered line of approach. The higher parts of the feature were wooded and partially planted with vineyards. This provided good cover, but it was essential to keep still: any movement would at once be detected. The tactical value of the feature was that it commanded the roads leading north and east from Agira, which were now the only means of escape for the Germans. The companies on Campanelli were entirely without support. A party carrying the 3-inch mortar and bombs reached them, but the man who was carrying the bipod legs had fallen behind and become lost. The mortars with the companies in the rear were useless owing to the range. There was no track at that time north of the Pyramids feature. The result was that all supplies had to be man-handled under cover of darkness. The absence of a track also prevented the Gunner O.P. from proceeding beyond the Pyramids, where the observation was quite useless, as the Campanelli feature rose several hundred feet higher.

The Germans were using their two escape roads from Agira

freely, and it was very tantalizing for the Hampshires not to be able to fire on the many excellent targets which presented themselves. It was obvious at first that the Germans had no idea that the Hampshires were waiting at the back door, but during the morning of 25th July their suspicions must have been aroused, for two patrols approached the Hampshire positions, were fired on and left casualties.

During the early part of the afternoon the Germans fired with guns and mortars on to the feature, and at about 1600 hrs. commenced to counter-attack the north end, which was held by " B " Company. There was some very fierce fighting at close range, in which the Hampshires suffered heavy casualties and " B " Company were compelled to withdraw. To meet such a contingency, " A " Company had prepared in advance a counter-attack, but Major H. D. Nelson Smith, who was in command of the two companies, decided that, against such strong opposition and without artillery support, such an attack could only end disastrously, and he decided to abandon Campanelli. Although the Hampshires' casualties on Campanelli were high and included Major M. D. Van Lessen, M.C., they would have been far higher had it not been for the skilful withdrawal conducted by Major H. D. Nelson Smith. Covered by successive lay-back positions of " A " Company, he withdrew the remnants of " B " Company right back to the Pyramids, and eventually " A " Company were withdrawn to a position behind " D " Company, who were immediately south of the road.

That night the Canadians decided to make another attack against Agira, and once again the Hampshires were asked to co-operate by pushing forward " D " and " A " Companies to the north side of the Agira—Regalbuto road, but this time they had strict instructions to withdraw at first light if the Canadian attack failed. The Dorsets also were asked to co-operate by attacking the feature 583, which lay to the south of and was entirely dominated by the heights of Agira.

Apart from the Hampshire and Dorset companies who were directly engaged in assisting the Canadian attack, the remainder of the Brigade Group remained static with forward positions on top of hills with their reserves and H.Qs. hugging the reverse slopes of the valleys. Perhaps the best impression of what it was like can be obtained from the following extract from the personal diary of the Intelligence Officer, who at that time visited each battalion in turn:

" *Morning, 25th July.*

"The Brigade Commander must think that I have

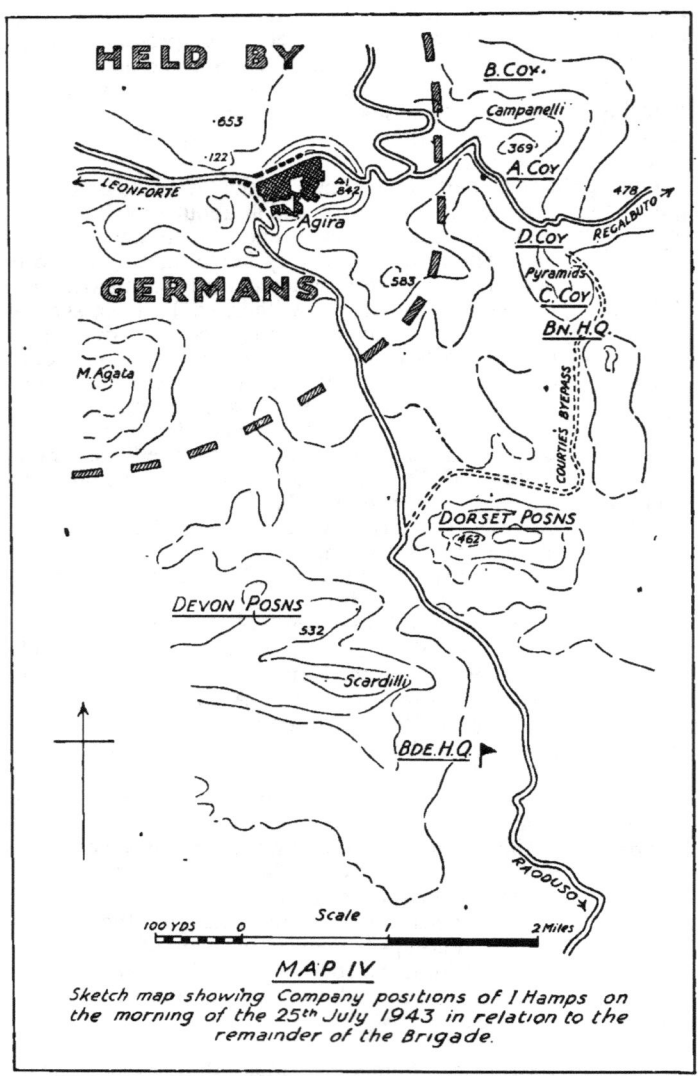

MAP IV

Sketch map showing Company positions of 1 Hamps on the morning of the 25th July 1943 in relation to the remainder of the Brigade.

nothing to do. He has ordered me to go and have a look at the Battalion positions. I am extremely annoyed about this because I always use these static periods to write intelligence summaries, bring the war diary up to date and clear off all the ' paper ' that has been received from Corps and Division. Now it will accumulate on me.

" Once I got over my annoyance I found myself looking forward to the prospect, and I decided to visit the forward platoons of the Dorsets.

" They are about a mile forward of us on the other side of the road—on top of a hell of a big hill called 462. It is going to be a strenuous walk—especially as I intend to circumvent that road even if it doubles the distance. Yesterday it was ' stonked ' at intervals of about a quarter of an hour.

" After a cross-country walk I found myself in the valley behind 462. The Germans seem to have changed their tactics to-day and they are searching these valleys— with their artillery—probably for headquarters and gun sites. A concentration has just come down behind the hill held by the Devons on the other side of the road.

" There's something coming over now. I go to ground— but the shells land some distance away—still across the road but nearer than before. I distinctly heard one large fragment whistle over my head. They seem to be working towards the valley so it behoves me to ' lift up mine eyes unto the hills.' Yes—I was right—the next packet fell not far away from the spot where I was standing ten minutes before.

" Christ! What a steep hill this is! I wonder how the Dorsets felt when they attacked it last night? They'll probably tell me when I get to the top. Here's the top now. Which company?—Dog. I lie with the men in holes on the summit. They are all anxious for news. Representatives from different groups crawl up to me and say, ' What's the gen, sir? ' I rack my brains and tell them everything I know, which is little enough—although some of it comes out of documents that are not supposed to go below the rank of Lieutenant-Colonel. However, they seem satisfied and crawl back to their friends—and I can see the news spreading like wildfire.

" Then someone brings a cup of tea. It astonishes me how there is always tea on the brew in places like this, while at Headquarters we never get more than three cups a day.

"Shells go over every few minutes and we duck, as of habit, for we are safe enough, as they are falling in the valley behind.

"It is grand up here in the sun—and what a view! Agira about two miles ahead—higher even than we are. It doesn't look possible to capture the place. And then the large plain between the town and us. It lies there like a model and every little feature can be seen by us—and even better by the Germans. Perhaps 'plain' is the wrong word because it is broken up by several distinct smaller hills. There is the hill which they call 583 immediately in front of Agira and dwarfed by those towering cliffs. Then to the right is the feature that the Hampshires have called the Pyramids. The reason is obvious now. It is the curious cutting of crops that gives the twin-topped hill a cubist appearance. Then there is the rough track across country to the Pyramids which the Sappers are making. Some call this Courtie's By-pass, but the Hampshires, of course, call it Hampshire Lane. There is not much concealment of our intention from the enemy there. It stands out a mile.

"I must be getting back. I wish this shelling would stop—I have to pass through that valley on my way home. Oh, well—here goes!

"I'm in the valley now—can I make it before the next lot?

"No, blast it! There's something coming over now—louder—louder—down. Crash! What a hell of a noise!

"I get up shaken—but intact—and peer through the dust. That was big stuff and near too—within fifty yards.

"Fortunately they fell in a fold in the ground and that protected me.

"I reckon that I have just time to sprint round that knoll before the next lot comes. Then I should be safe. I wish I was in better training.

"*Afternoon, 25th July.*

"'Would you like to come with me to visit the Hampshires?' said the Old Man.

"'Yes, sir—rather!' said I heartily, hoping that my voice carried conviction.

"Soon we are off in the jeep. Everything seems quiet. Only the jeep moves. Round the bend of the road we come across a damaged German gun.

"'88-mm,' said the Old Man.

THE VIEW FROM THE GERMAN O.P. AT AGIRA.

[Crown Copyright Reserved

" ' No, sir—their new 75 anti-tank gun—it's the first I've seen.'

" And my morale improved enormously at this demonstration of my superior knowledge.

" After a while we leave the road and traverse the open country on Courtie's Bypass.

" My mind is full of mixed feelings. I keep wondering—why the hell doesn't Jerry fire at us?—he must be able to see us from the tip of Agira. And I find the words of an old rag-time song repeating over and over again in my brain:

' You ought to sit with Hannah in a big armchair,
It's like going through Alaska in your underwear.'

" It must be the association of ideas and this nightmare feeling of nakedness.

" The Old Man does not seem to bother at all. He just drives steadily on.

" From time to time we meet men of the Support Company mortars and odd parties of Sappers.

" The Brigadier stops and talks to them all and I find myself thinking what a sense of security his presence there must give to them.

" I brace my shoulders and try to make myself look something more than a reluctant shadow of the great man.

" Soon we reach the Hampshires' Headquarters.

" They are on the reverse side of the Pyramids near a ruined farmhouse. They are well dug in—and no wonder—for the Jerries have this place taped. All around are the marks of shells and mortar bombs.

" It is very quiet and peaceful, but we don't stay long. The Brigadier sees Colonel Spencer and says what has to be said.

" One bad bit of news as we leave. Something has happened to the Hampshires' forward companies on Campanelli to the right of Agira and they are being forced to evacuate.

" The journey back seems twice as long as the journey out and my back seems terribly exposed. I expect to hear a burst of machine-gun fire at any moment.

" The Brigadier stops only once—to assist a despatch rider whose vehicle has broken down.

" He stops bang on the skyline.

" At such times as these the words of the military pamphlet on ' Taking Cover and Use of the Ground ' are burned into my soul with letters of burnished gold.

"*Afternoon, 26th July.*

"Having nothing to do, for once, I thought I'd beat the Old Man to it.

"' May I visit the Devons this afternoon, sir? ' I said.

"' Yes, certainly,' he replied, looking pleased and, I thought, somewhat surprised.

"I called in at the Devons' Headquarters on the way.

"' You're not going to walk all the way? ' said Colonel Valentine. ' At least use my carrier to the top of that hill.'

"So I set off with John Symes, the Signal Officer, who wanted to repair some damaged lines and who promised to act as guide.

"The carrier could not proceed far. Soon the rocky crest of Scardelli confronted us and we got out and started to climb.

"Over the top and down into a deep valley. It is very hot and I perspire freely. There is not the slightest suggestion of war about the scene.

"Threading our way through a farmyard we proceed to climb the hill where the Devons' forward companies are entrenched. I estimate that we have to climb about a thousand feet.

"Up and up, until we come to Captain Duke and his company. They are dug in on the reverse slope just behind the crest. There is little to show that earlier this had been the scene of bloody fighting. Only some captured enemy machine guns and a mound with a wooden cross on it, partly hidden by the cactus—the grave of one of our men.

"They are in great spirits and seemed pleased to see me.

"There is the usual request for news—and I oblige as well as I am able. Their only complaint is that it is difficult to get rations and water up. There is some jealousy of the company on the left who have captured a civilian who brings them vino.

"Hearing of this—I decide to visit that company.

"Before I leave, ' Bubbles ' Duke hands me a German newspaper. It is a fairly recent one and contains the German version of the attack on Sicily. The Germans say we took them by surprise, but that they will soon beat us back to the beaches.

"It was ' Dog ' Company that lay over on the left about

half a mile distant and on the forward slope. First I met Capt. ' Mike ' Holdsworth.

" He took me into a small farmhouse and the inevitable cup of tea was produced.

" We chat and I tell him all the news and point out the disposition of our troops on the ground.

" There is an air of complete unreality about the scene and this is increased as Major ' Ron ' Biggart approaches with a walking-stick.

" More than ever he looks like the squire who owns these broad acres.

" A patrol consisting of an officer and two men left this company this morning in an attempt to find the enemy ammunition dump. Nothing has since been heard of them and we search the ground with our binoculars to see if we can notice any sign of movement.

" While we are doing this a heavy mortar barrage starts to come down on the hill known as 583. It seems strange watching it at this safe distance.

" ' Have we anyone there? ' asks the Major.

" ' Yes,' I reply, ' the Dorsets.'

" But there is nothing we can do about it. The Brigade dispositions in this area are fantastic.

" And so I decided to return home. It is a long walk—three miles of hills and valleys—but it has been worth it. I have enjoyed this afternoon."

The attacks on Hill 583 which the I.O. recalls in his diary were made against only one Dorset platoon, although both " A " and " B " Companies of the Dorsets had been on or near the feature previously with the object of covering the work of the Sappers, who were trying to extend the track to the Agira—Regalbuto road. Apart from this, during the past two days the Dorsets' activity was confined to patrols which were led by Lieuts. E. Hannah, Brown and Lushington.

At 2000 hrs. on 26th July the 1st Canadian Division made their third attempt to capture Agira. Once again the Hampshires were ordered to cross the road and the Dorsets to capture Hill 583, and then send a strong fighting patrol forward to a road junction near Agira. The Canadians determined to support their attack with all the artillery fire they could muster and the 165 Field Regiment was taken away from us and transferred to the Leonforte area. Although they supported us together with other Canadian artillery in the attacks which were made later, the 165 Field Regiment was not returned to our exclusive command until the fighting in Sicily was finished.

It is perhaps convenient at this point to pay to the 165 Field Regiment, R.A., the tribute which they deserve. While they were with us they were brilliantly commanded by Major R. S. Osmond, who had to take over the command at short notice from Lieut.-Colonel Awdrey just before we left Egypt. Everyone was delighted when, on the return of Lieut.-Colonel Awdrey, Major Osmond was given the command of a regiment of his own. It is difficult to know what to say about the 165 Field Regiment. They were not in the limelight like the forward companies of battalions, but they were always there behind us when we wanted them, and this by itself was no mean feat, as the Gunners' transport difficulties were acute. As the battalions moved forward so did the Gunners also move, but what few of the infantry realized was that it took them twenty-four hours of hard ferrying to bring up all the ammunition to the new positions. Nevertheless, their fire was always there when called for, and it was accurate fire. The 165 Field Regiment had none of the Malta associations that bound together the three battalions, but they fitted into the Brigade Group right from the start, and they were distressed whenever operational or administrative reasons compelled them to separate from us. The officers and men of the 165 Field Regiment have frequently expressed their liking for the Malta Brigade, and this could only be equalled by the admiration which we had of their courage and skill.

The third attack of the Canadians was no more successful than the other two. The Hampshires and the Dorsets carried out their part of the contract as usual, but were compelled to withdraw from positions which were impossible to hold during daylight. The Dorsets and Devons still continued to send forward patrols, but the Hampshires had been so weakened by the fighting of the past three days and nights that they could now raise only three rifle companies. The Brigade Commander therefore decided to withdraw them from their positions round the Pyramids and they went into reserve behind the Devons and Dorsets.

Although we were under command of the Canadian Division, we had not yet met the Canadians, but we were not happy in our solitude. Our position south of Agira was extremely insecure and had remained so for a week, while the Canadians were unable to remedy the matter. During the time while we had been assisting their attacks on Agira, those officers who had access to the casualty returns had seen our casualties rise by about 300.

CHAPTER X

"CHANGE DIRECTION RIGHT"

AT MIDDAY ON 27TH JULY it became known that the Canadians were to make a fourth attempt to capture Agira, and the Brigade Commander held a conference at which the Devons were ordered to occupy firstly Point 583 and the Campanelli feature. Having thus secured a firm base astride the Agira—Regalbuto road, the Dorsets were to pass through to the road on the right of the Devons and then drive on to Regalbuto. The Dorsets were to have the support of " A " Squadron of the Royal Canadian Tank Regiment, a platoon of 66 Field Company, R.E., a troop of 300 Anti-Tank Battery, and a section of 4.2-inch mortars from the Brigade Support Company. The point of the Devons capturing 583 was to cover the work of the Sappers during the night. The Sappers were making every effort to lengthen the track until it met the Regalbuto road. The Devons' move to Campanelli was only possible if the Sappers' work had been completed. The addition of the Canadian tanks to our force was very welcome. Our own squadron had been taken away from us after the assault on the beaches at Marzamemi. Up to Vizzini we had been covered by the tanks of the 23rd Armoured Brigade, but from that time onwards we had been thrusting deep into the heart of enemy territory with " soft skin " vehicles only. Had we been strongly counter-attacked by enemy tanks we would have had to rely entirely on the anti-tank guns of battalions and the 300 Anti-Tank Battery. The country round Agira was not really suitable for tanks, but there had been occasions when the infantry had been compelled to gain ground by desperate commando tactics when a squadron of tanks could have easily butted their way through. The increase in morale of having once again tanks working side by side with the infantry could clearly be seen during the next few days of fighting.

The original plan was to develop the track past the 583 feature during the night, but the Sapper officer who went forward with an escort to make a reconnaissance found that the route was intersected by deep wadis, and the project was abandoned. Therefore it was decided to develop Courtie's Bypass which already led to the Pyramid feature.

Prior to making their attack on Campanelli, the Devons sent forward a reconnaissance patrol under Sergt. Brooking. He returned with an excellent report. The hill was held by six machine guns, five on the western slopes and one on the east. In view of the strength of the position the Brigade Commander offered Lieut.-Colonel Valentine the support of some of the tanks, and this was at once accepted. " C " Company of the Devons were detailed to make the attack and Capt. Duke was told to get as near to the enemy position as possible and then wait for the tank and artillery support.

The situation on the morning of the 28th was as follows:

The Devons were holding the 583 feature, but had not moved towards Campanelli because the Sappers had made little progress during the night. " C " Company of the Dorsets had moved forward and were thought to be in the vicinity of the Regalbuto road east of the Campanelli feature. At 0930 hrs. General Simmonds visited Brigade Headquarters. He stated that the Canadians had cleared all enemy opposition away from the west of Agira, and that the position was now favourable for our advance on Regalbuto. The Brigade Commander immediately went forward to find out the exact position of our troops, and once again the best record of the situation, as it existed at that time, is found in the personal diary of the Intelligence Officer:

"*Morning, 28th July*

" General Simmonds of the 1st Canadian Division has just called at Brigade H.Q. It appears that the last attack of the Canadians has been more successful. They have cleared all enemy opposition to the west of Agira. In fact, by now they should be on the point of entering the town.

" Our orders are to get astride the Agira—Regalbuto road and then attack in the direction of Regalbuto. The Dorsets are reported to have a company in the vicinity of the road, and the Brigadier has decided to go forward with me and find out what is happening.

" The Brigade Group has been fighting continuously now for about ten days. Sometimes they are small actions, sometimes large, but always the situation changes and I find that unless I get forward at least once a day it is quite impossible to keep a grip on things.

" Once again we are on Courtie's Bypass. It still feels horribly exposed, but there is more traffic about to-day. Carriers and anti-tank guns are moving forward. Soon we outstrip this slow-moving traffic and approach the rear end of the Pyramid feature.

" A series of explosions can be heard ahead. We are screened by a fold in the ground and it is impossible to see what is happening. We see Capt. Whitehead, the Brigade

E.M.E., sheltering behind a pile of stones and attempting to recover a damaged vehicle.

" 'That's German mortar fire across the track,' he said.

" 'Don't go on just yet; it's certain to stop in a few minutes.' But I know that the Brigade Commander will take no notice of this. It is essential that we should push on quickly. So we drive on, and I endeavour to compose my thoughts, but I fear the worst.

" As we come round the Pyramids and into the open we see three vehicles burning merrily. One contains ammunition and this sends out a series of small explosions. The drivers of the vehicles are taking cover about a hundred yards away.

" Now—I think to myself—is the time. Step on it and we will soon be past this unhealthy spot.

" But the Old Man drives steadily on and then—to my utter dismay—stops dead in the middle of the vehicles.

" I am terrified. This, I feel, is not in my contract. These vehicles have obviously been knocked out by a tank or anti-tank gun. I expect a shell to turn us into a fourth conflagration at any moment.

" One of the vehicles—a jeep—has a huge Brigade sign propped up in the back seat. It faces the enemy and must be visible for over a mile through binoculars. The third vehicle belongs to our police and contains a load of direction signs. The Brigadier thinks that this can be recovered, as only the wheels are on fire. He shouts to the driver and we attempt to get it going, but the ignition has gone.

" Suddenly there is another explosion behind us. The popular opinion is that it is more ammo exploding, but I am not so sure. I thought I heard the whistle after the strike which is the sure sign of a high-velocity gun.

" We decide to move on. We have only been on the spot for about five minutes. It feels like days.

" Soon we are moving along the front side of the Pyramids. Shell fire seems to be following us—about 200 yards behind and slightly higher up the hill. If it does catch up with us there is a reasonable chance that it will be over our heads.

" There is still no sign of the Dorset company. A Sapper sergeant tells us that his company have been compelled to suspend work on the track owing to mortar fire. I can see the Brigade Commander beginning to get a little irritated.

We leave the jeep in charge of the wireless operator and proceed on foot.

" In the direction of the Regalbuto road, mortar fire is coming down. It is cross-fire from both flanks.

" Then across the valley we see two soldiers. Even through binoculars it is difficult to distinguish whether they are ours or the enemy—but they are probably ours, because that is where the Dorsets should be situated.

" I am afraid that the Brigadier will get back in his car and drive on and be captured, so I offer to make a reconnaissance on foot. He agrees.

" I make a careful note of the position and set off.

" Soon I am floundering about in deep wadis among trees and prickly-pear bushes. Even in the day time I find it difficult to keep direction. God knows how the battalions attack over country like this at night.

" This distance is much farther than I anticipated, but eventually I get out of the wadis and catch a glimpse of the two soldiers. They are ours and are firing a 3-inch mortar.

" They are supporting the Dorset company, who are taking cover behind a terrace and under a thick hedge of prickly pear. A sergeant is in charge and he explains that they are held up. There is an open stretch of ground between them and the road and this is covered by enemy machine-gun fire. Capt. Martin is in command of the company. He had seen the Brigadier across the valley and had gone back to report the situation. We must have crossed without seeing each other.

" So I return only to find that the Brigadier and the jeep have disappeared. There is nothing for me to do except make my way down the track on foot."

When the Brigade I.O. eventually caught up with the Brigadier the confusion had been cleared and the battle set in motion again. The Brigade Commander had decided to assist the Dorset company forward by attacks on either flank. The attack on the left flank was against the Campanelli feature and was made by the Devons as prearranged. Tanks could not move over the rough ground of Campanelli, but they were able to take hull-down positions on the left of " C " Company. The movement forward of the tanks was covered by an artillery barrage and the tanks in their turn covered the forward movement of the infantry.

It was a fine attack that was made by Capt. Duke and the men of " C " Company, and by some very close fighting they flung the enemy from their stronghold, and more Germans were killed than were taken prisoner. After the Devons had secured the feature they were attacked from a distance by German tanks, but the Brigade Support Company came to their assistance with the heavy mortars. Lieut. P. N. Cox had been making a reconnaissance for an approach for anti-tank guns while the attack was in progress. He succeeded in getting 6-pounders up a very difficult route and into position. We had got a firm grip on Campanelli at last.

Meantime " D " Company of the Dorsets were attacking on the right. Despite the fact that they were heavily sniped by Italians concealed in the thick undergrowth and by some mischance were fired on by our own artillery, this attack went well. The squadron of tanks assisted in the final stages and over 80 prisoners were captured by the company. Bdsn. Maloney, who was with " D " Company, displayed great courage in attending to the wounded under fire until he himself lost his life.

The success of these actions permitted the remainder of the Devon and Dorset battalions to move forward and by last light the Dorsets were securely astride the road with four infantry companies in box formation. Behind them on Campanelli, to the south of the road, and on 583 the Devons were providing a firm base.

The plan for the following morning was that the attack should continue towards Regalbuto on a two-battalion front with the Hampshires to the left of the road and the Dorsets to the right. Some valuable information was received from civilian sources, which indicated that the next serious opposition could be expected much nearer Regalbuto. This proved to be correct, and with only slight enemy opposition and demolitions to contend with the two battalions made good progress for the next two miles. In the early afternoon, however, stiffer opposition was encountered and a full-scale attack had to be planned. Once again the diary describes the situation:

" *Afternoon, 29th July.*

" After selecting a site for Brigade H.Q. I returned to see how the battle was progressing.

" The demolished bridge which is holding up our progress has been made passable by the bulldozer and I am able to proceed about a mile farther up the road until I come to the top of a hill where the road crosses the crest in a cutting. There is a tremendous congestion of traffic here; tanks and carriers are stopped practically touching each other.

"Proceeding on foot through the cutting I see the country open out in front of me and obtain my first view of Regalbuto.

"An action is in progress. The Dorsets are attacking a large hill on the right of the road. On the map this is called Stupari. At the same time, the Hampshires are attacking the lower ground to the left of the road. Nothing can be seen of the troops of either battalion, as the ground is far too broken and wooded.

"There is a tremendous noise as, from time to time, the tanks come out of the cutting and fire at the ground in front of the Hampshires with everything they have got. I can see their tracer fire searching the area.

"Battles are usually disappointing spectacles, but this scene might have been set by Hollywood. The tanks have no cover—they are in full view. Their tracer fire is like a firework display and in the noise it is almost impossible to hear oneself speak.

"Also on the road and in full view of the enemy is the Brigade Commander and round him the C.Os. of the three battalions and Lieut.-Colonel Awdrey of the 165 Field Regiment. They are in a magnificent position to direct operations, but one enemy shell would wipe out the lot.

"On the outside of the group are Staff officers, liaison officers and war correspondents. I have a long talk with Major Lewis Hastings, the B.B.C. commentator. I have always found him worth listening to, but now, as he agrees with everything I say, my opinion of him is higher than ever. He is a sick man to-day and from time to time he doubles up in a ditch.

"A short time afterwards a shout comes from the higher ground on the left. 'We've captured our objective!' It is Colonel Ray.

"'Well done, Dorsets,' replies the Brigade Commander. Nothing has been heard from the Hampshires. The Brigadier sends me forward to Colonel Spencer to find out the news. I soon find him—but he also is in the dark. His troops have disappeared into the undergrowth and he is afraid that if the tanks continue firing it will be ourselves and not the enemy who will suffer casualties.

"It is some time before we hear that the Hampshires are on their objective, which is two rocky mounds which project from the low ground to the left of the road.

" It looks a very insecure position, especially as mortar fire has commenced to come down in that area."

The Dorsets had done well to capture their objective, which was a huge hill with a commanding view over the whole Regalbuto area. Capt. Chilton, of " B " Company, had particularly distinguished himself. As his company struggled up the lower slopes of the steep hill they came under intense machine-gun and mortar fire which caused many casualties. Capt. Chilton, having got his company under cover, went forward himself to make a reconnaissance. He then put in his attack, leading his company with great dash and determination. He was the first man into the enemy positions and by the use of his revolver and hand grenades personally accounted for several of the German defenders.

It was now quite obvious that only one feature remained to be captured before the town of Regalbuto fell into our hands. This was a long ridge (afterwards known as Regalbuto Ridge) which lay on the south side of parallel to the road. It was decided that the Hampshires should attack the ridge that night.

It is interesting to make a contrast between the road that led from Raodusa to Agira and the Agira—Regalbuto road. The former was completely dominated by Agira itself; every movement along it for miles could be clearly seen by the enemy, and the German guns made full use of the observation. The other road was very different. Regalbuto was lower than many points on it, and there were large areas that provided dead ground and safe positions. There were other stretches of road, however, that were fully exposed to view, and it so happened that in these places movement off the road was quite impossible.

By this time the Germans were either short of artillery or short of ammunition, and they adapted their tactics to make the best use of their limited resources. Movement on the open stretches of the road was always liable to bring down artillery fire, but the Germans usually waited for a target which was worth their while. They must have given careful study to this road and made careful registration. They had selected about six places which were probable concentration areas and these they subjected to harassing fire at intervals of about half an hour. Brigade Tac. H.Q., the liaison officers, despatch riders and all other persons whose duties took them backwards and forwards to the forward companies knew these danger spots only too well. Lieut. Elliot, Brigade Liaison Officer, was passing through one of these dangerous places when a shell hit the road in front of him. He was screened by a tank and no damage was done.

Later in the same day he was going up the hill to Agira when another shell burst in front of him, killing four Canadians. Much of their firing was done by 88-mm. guns, which were primarily intended as anti-tank or anti-aircraft weapons. A fire plan of one of these guns was afterwards captured which showed that the targets had been selected as far away as 11,000 metres and as near as 500 yards.

This German shelling gave us our best laugh at the expense of the Brigade Support Company. This unit had not been properly formed when we left Egypt, and throughout the Sicilian campaign Major Richard Langrishe, who commanded, had been building it up by bits and pieces. He had captured enemy weapons and vehicles and was particularly proud of one Diesel-driven tractor and trailer. Among other things, he had acquired a complete farmyard, consisting of chickens, bees and a pig. He had the habit of calling in at Brigade H.Q. and telling us how much better was the site he had selected than was our own. On this occasion we were inclined to believe him, as we were rather exposed. " My position has everything," said Major Langrishe. " Water, fruit and cover—the Germans know I am there all right, but they just can't get at me." About an hour later he returned. His moustache was bristling and his eyes glistening with fury. " The Boche," he said, " the bloody Boche has burnt my beautiful trailer and hundreds of gallons of Diesel oil have gone up in smoke. I wouldn't mind that so much but the hens have been killed, all my bees have flown away, and the pig has b——d off in the blitz."

CHAPTER XI

REGALBUTO RIDGE

A FEATURE OF THE COUNTRY between Agira and Regalbuto was its suitability for defensive warfare. It was quite impossible by the usual reconnaissance methods to spot the enemy positions in the closely wooded and mountainous country. A succession of ridges running at right angles to the road offered a choice of defensive positions which the Germans used to the full. Their method of fighting rearguard actions in this type of country was to get the Italians to dig the positions and so rest themselves before the actual fighting. They would then lie very low until our troops approached to within a few yards, when they would open up with many automatic weapons. Our forces would withdraw to reorganize, but often after a second full-scale attack was made against the same positions they would be found to be vacated. When this happened the situation would be exactly the reverse. The Germans knew exactly where we were, because we were holding their old positions, with the result that heavy shelling and mortar fire would come down on our troops from previous registration.

Not all ridges were defended. Sometimes a big attack with artillery barrage would be made against a piece of country that was entirely unoccupied. At other times a small force like a company would attack a position in which it was found that the enemy were firmly entrenched. Something like this happened when the first attack was made on Regalbuto Ridge by the Hampshires. This attack was made after a long period of dogged fighting by the battalion round Agira, and took place on the night of the second day of the two-day advance from Agira. So far as anyone knew at that time, it was just another objective to be captured by the Hampshires during the night. It was not realized that this was the dominating feature of the whole Regalbuto position, and that it was here that the Germans had chosen to make their stand to prevent the capture of Regalbuto, a keypoint in the defensive line covering their withdrawal from Sicily.

For once luck was against the Hampshires. They were caught by fire from six-barrelled Nebelwerfers on the start line, and the huge projectiles caused great damage, practically wiping out one platoon and sapping the determination of the others. Nevertheless, the Hampshires pushed forward bravely, only to be caught in the cross-fire of machine guns whose presence was not suspected. The casualties were now so high and the distance gained towards the objective so small, that it became obvious that the attack could not succeed, and so it was called off and the troops withdrawn.

When morning came it was possible to have a better look at the ridge. It was on the south of the road running from Agira to Regalbuto. It was a long ridge and, unlike the rest of the country, it ran parallel to the road and not at right angles. It contained three distinct features and gradually rose in height to a point immediately south of the town of Regalbuto. Its greatest height was just under 2,000 feet.

At midday on 30th July the Brigade Commander held a conference on a vantage point to the left of the road in the area

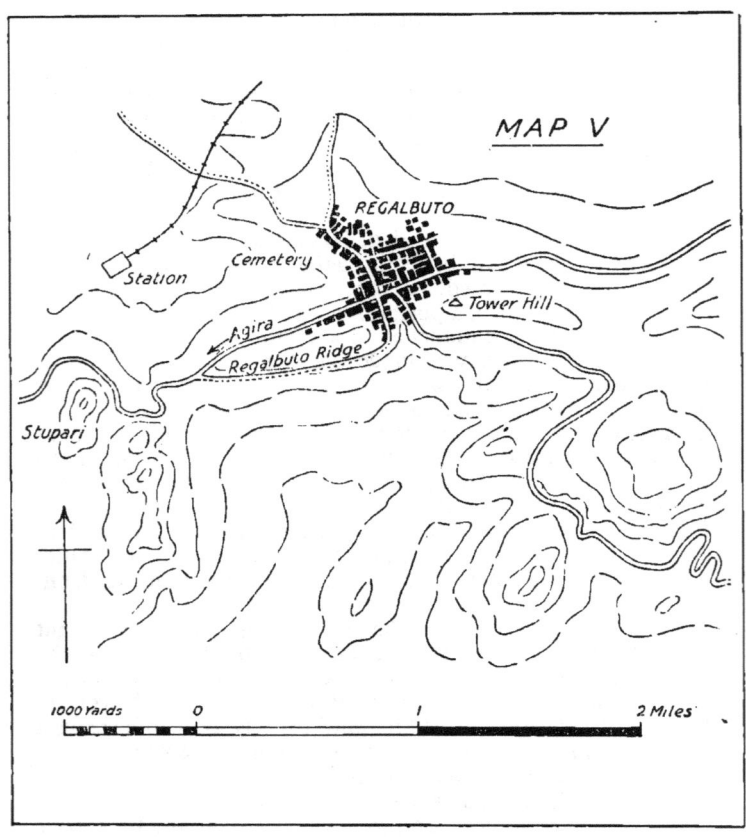

known as Petteruta. This place was used as an O.P. by 165 Field Regiment and the 1st Canadian Field Regiment. The road ran in a defile close by and it was well "taped" by the German guns, who "stonked" it periodically. The road about 100 yards to the right of the conference place was shelled frequently during the meeting, causing everyone except the Brigade Commander to lie low—he continued leaning nonchalantly against a tree.

The plan outlined at that conference was that Regalbuto Ridge should be attacked by the Devons with the support of all artillery under command of the 1st Canadian Division. This comprised four field regiments and three medium regiments—a total of 144 guns. In view of the natural strength of the position, Lieut.-Colonel Valentine asked that the attack should be made at night and from the northern flank instead of from the front.

The disadvantage of attacking the feature from the flank was that it entailed a difficult approach march in the dark for a distance of approximately two miles. The preliminary reconnaissance over this area was made by Lieut. F. A. Pearson, who with one of his sections went out in daylight to select the route with a view to guiding the battalion at night. He succeeded in getting to within 200 yards of the right flank of the enemy positions, which were found to extend from the Regalbuto Ridge across the road to the north.

All day long the registration of targets by the guns continued and shoots were made by the Hampshire mortars and guns of the 1st Canadian Field Regiment on an area which a patrol of the Hampshires had revealed as occupied by the enemy. A certain amount of machine-gun fire was exchanged by the Germans and the Dorsets on the right flank.

That night, shortly before the artillery concentrations were due to begin, the Brigade Commander and the Brigade Intelligence Officer went to the same feature where the conference had been held and where the Devons had now established their main Battalion H.Q. Soon the guns opened up and there was a considerable swishing sound as the shells passed overhead to burst on Regalbuto Ridge in flickering points of light. It was by far the heaviest artillery concentration which had been used in any of our attacks so far. Something had gone wrong with the wireless sets of the forward companies, and Capt. Holdsworth, Adjutant of the Devons, was unable to get any news from his C.O., who was forward with Tac. H.Q. After the barrage lifted some spasmodic firing was heard—first the quick splutter of the Spandau and the steady rat-tat-tat of the Bren, and we knew that the assaulting troops had made contact. Then followed a long and anxious wait of nearly an hour, during which time nothing was heard of the progress of the battle. Finally at 0147 hrs. three red Very lights were seen to be fired from the ridge, which indicated that the right of the objective had been taken. At 0235 hrs. the success signal—three green lights—came from the left of the objective. Regalbuto Ridge was in our hands.

The plan now was to get the Devon transport, and particularly the carriers, forward and down the road to the ridge. It was known that a bridge had been demolished on this road and the

Sappers were ready with a bulldozer to effect repairs. The progress of this bulldozer could be heard for miles in the stillness of the night and as soon as it approached the demolished bridge a German anti-tank gun fired on fixed lines—bursts of two shots every few minutes. Major Courtie reported the hold-up and he and the Brigade Commander went forward to the bridge. It was possible to stand quite close to this bridge in safety and hear the anti-tank shells go swishing by to crack into the hillside beyond. It was decided that if the anti-tank gun ceased firing for a period of fifteen minutes the bulldozer should make another attempt. This never did happen until just before dawn, when the crew of the anti-tank gun, which proved to be an 88-mm., pulled out after first destroying the piece. The bulldozer quickly repaired the damaged bridge, and transport started passing over—the first vehicle to cross the bridge being the Brigadier's jeep. Thus contact was re-established with the Devons on the ridge.

Until then nothing was known of the progress of the attack except that it had obviously gone in late. Here is the story as told by Lieut.-Colonel Valentine, M.B.E.:

"At 2100 hrs. the battalion left its area, led by ' B ' Company, whose objective was the eastern or far end of the ridge. Then came ' A ' Company, who were going for the centre and western end. Battalion Tac. H.Q. and ' D ' Company brought up the rear of the column. ' D ' Company were to be directed on to the rear end of the ridge if the attack was successful, or used to assist the other companies, if required. ' C ' Company in reserve were left behind near the main road with two 6-pounder portees and one 3-ton lorry standing by to carry the company forward up the main road when the objectives had been captured. Also ready to move up were all the mortar carriers, anti-tank guns and one carrier per company with ammunition, food and water. These arrangements were made, as the route taken by the battalion was quite impossible for transport. In fact, in this area it was quite out of the question to move even tracked vehicles any distance from the main road.

"The column wound its way silently in single file across country, which proved to be even more difficult than had been anticipated, entailing as it did a climb down a precipitous slope which proved too much for wireless sets, which all went out of action.

"The enemy realized that an attack was imminent, and heavy defensive fire, both artillery and mortar, was brought down. They expected the attack from the front, however, and the battalion moved round the flank of this fire and eventually between it and the enemy positions.

" ' B ' Company advanced towards their objective but encountered a tank on the main road which was moving up and down and obviously firing at any sound it heard. One platoon had a number of casualties. Capt. G. P. Spread very ably led the other two platoons round between the tank and the town and got on his objective at about 0200 hrs. Below them they could hear tanks moving on the road and in the town, and the constant sound of large bodies of troops marching to and fro. Words of command could be clearly heard.

" In the meantime ' A ' Company had also advanced on its objective, capturing on the way a 22-mm. dual-purpose anti-aircraft and anti-tank gun which was found to be trained on the spot where the Brigade Commander had met his commanding officers on the morning before. The crew threw a few grenades and ran. After some sharp fighting the objective was captured. The position was found to be a strong one, covered by deep slit trenches and commanding all the approaches from the west.

" The Commanding Officer then moved Battalion Tac. H.Q. and ' D ' Company on to the western end of the ridge and sent back for ' C ' Company to come up. He then went along the ridge to contact the forward companies. ' A ' Company were digging in in a firm position which they could hold against strong attack. ' B ' Company had only got two platoons up, and in view of the movement that could be heard below on the road and in the town he told Capt. Spread that he would send up a platoon from the reserve company to help him out. This was done, but unfortunately this platoon was held up *en route* by a hidden Spandau and did not arrive on the forward end of the ridge in time to influence the battle which was to take place later.

" The position of the companies along the ridge from front to rear was now as follows: ' B ' Company in the most forward position; ' A ' Company on the centre feature; ' C ' Company, less one platoon, on a subsidiary feature in rear of ' A ' Company, and ' D ' Company on the western end. In front of ' B ' Company and to the south-east of the town stood Tower Hill, a steep and rocky hill with a ruined tower on its summit which gave it its name and which later was found to be a German O.P. Lieut. Pearson had sent a patrol forward consisting of Sergt. Collett and one man to see if this was occupied, and they soon returned stating that there was no doubt that the enemy was there and also between them and Tower Hill.

"Capt. Spread at first light expressed his intention of going tank hunting, and with C.S.M. Jones, his Company H.Q. and one section with two Brens, worked his way down the side of the hill and engaged the tanks—a very brave and gallant act. Capt. Spread was himself firing a Bren gun when one of the men shouted, ' They are turning their big guns on us.' The tanks at once opened fire with H.E. and this was the end of the gallant little party, who all became casualties. Capt. Spread and the C.S.M. and several other men were killed and all the remainder wounded."

About this time the Brigade Commander and the Brigade Intelligence Officer arrived at Battalion H.Q. on the rear end of Regalbuto Ridge. Ordering the I.O. to remain behind, the Brigade Commander went forward with Lieut.-Colonel Valentine to investigate the position. While they were away a German counter-attack developed and " D " Company, who were close by Headquarters, received orders to move forward to resist this attack. Such was the size and length of Regalbuto Ridge that it was not realized at the rear end of the ridge that such fierce fighting was taking place at the front. The full light of daylight was needed to show that the feature captured was really much more than a battalion objective, and that the men must of necessity be very thin on the ground, especially this battalion, which by that time was under strength by about 200 men owing to casualties sustained since Vizzini.

Realizing the seriousness of the position, the Brigade Commander returned to organize reinforcements—shortly to be followed by the I.O. The most reliable story of the action again therefore comes from the pen of the Colonel :

"The situation on the eastern end of the ridge, where No. 12 Platoon under Lieut. Pearson was in the most forward position, had deteriorated. They had seen tanks in the village and the crews observing them through glasses. The tanks had then opened fire with H.E. and under cover of their fire the German shock troops, who subsequently proved to be the Hermann Goering Engineers and Paratroops, had climbed up the hill on all sides, their strength in this area being about two companies. As they approached they shouted out ' All right, Charlie, Canadians.' Practically the whole forward platoon became casualties after hand-to-hand fighting with much grenade throwing on both sides, and the remainder of ' B ' Company, now very much reduced in strength, was driven off the forward position.

" ' A ' Company held firm on their feature, and ' C ' Company, under Capt. H. V. Duke, were moved up to stop the German advance. This they did, and the situation now was that ' A ' and ' C ' Companies were in very close contact with the enemy, the distance not being more than seventy yards.

" The Germans were working in pairs, each having a Spandau and a machine pistol, with a plentiful supply of ammunition. They acted individually and not as sections, infiltrating forward whenever they got a chance, and climbing along the wooded slopes of the hill and continually appearing in unexpected places. They were well trained, young and active, their average age not being more than 19 or 20. Ammunition in ' A ' and ' C ' Companies was now getting low. All their grenades and 2-inch mortar ammunition had been expended and the L.M.G. were down to two or three magazines per gun. The Commanding Officer decided to use ' D ' Company to drive the enemy finally from the ridge. He brought up Major T. R. Biggart, M.B.E., with ' D ' Company and put them in round the right flank. The Germans at once started to withdraw and all along the lines there, were shouts of ' They're going! ' Men got up fixing bayonets and cheering and the enemy were finally driven off the position at the point of the bayonet.

" During the counter-attack Major Biggart was wounded and Lieut. G. F. H. Arundell killed, leaving no officers in ' D ' Company. C.S.M. Bollam, M.B.E., took command, captured his objective and reorganized the company, reinforced by the Intelligence Section and other odd parties which were sent forward to assist in holding what was the keypoint of the whole position."

Throughout the Sicilian campaign Brigade Tac. H.Q. had been a small mobile party consisting of the Brigade Commander and the Brigade I.O. in a jeep and one or more liaison officers of the Brigade in a jeep or on motor-cycles. Contact was maintained with the forward companies either personally or through liaison officer—the wireless being used principally to keep the Brigade Major informed of the situation at Advance Brigade H.Q. Such methods gave great impetus to the attack—but never were they to prove themselves so valuable as on the only occasion that we were on the defensive.

The Brigade Commander twice visited the Devons during the action and was in close touch with everything that was happening. He sent up " C " Company of the 1st Hampshires to take over " D " Company's position, and a strong platoon of the Brigade Support Company under Lieut. Turner came up as a valuable reserve on the western end of the ridge.

As far as the Devons were concerned, the position on top of the ridge was now stabilized, although Regalbuto Ridge was to remain a dangerous place for the next two days. On the same afternoon the Dorsets made attacks on either side of the ridge and met considerable opposition.

By the time that the Brigade Group had reached Regalbuto Ridge the Support Company had begun to show great skill in the handling of their 4.2-inch mortars. We began to feel that at distances of around 3,000 yards we had, at last, something to compete with the German mortars, which we held in great respect. The officers in charge of our 4.2-inch mortars were particularly dashing in siting their O.Ps. so far forward. On Regalbuto Ridge their O.P. was with the forward Devon platoons, and the desire to provide his mortars with the best possible observation cost the life of Lieut. E. Helps, one of our best officers.

The capture and subsequent defence of Regalbuto Ridge were a great personal triumph for Lieut.-Colonel Valentine, M.B.E., the Commanding Officer of the 2nd Devons. It was his plan of attack from the flank over difficult country that was responsible for the taking of the position. Later, when counter-attacked, he disposed his troops in such a way that they were able to hold an area that would usually be considered too large for one battalion. He had proved himself a great leader of men, instilling great confidence in the troops under his command, and at the height of the battle he had taken up a tommy-gun himself and led them forward against the enemy.

The Devons' casualties for that day were 8 officers and 101 other ranks. Capt. H. V. Duke was wounded in the shoulder by a grenade but refused to withdraw until the situation had been restored. That meant that all the Devon rifle company commanders who had landed in Sicily were now out of action—either killed or wounded. Capt. M. W. Howard, who commanded the anti-tank platoon, was also wounded in the head when he had gone forward to assist the other companies. After his wounds had been dressed he came back to the fight again and materially helped to make up for the shortage of officers by moving from one threatened point to another, preventing enemy infiltration and encouraging the men to further efforts.

Many acts of bravery were seen that day among the Devon men and the names of Sergt. R. Collett and Cpl. Gizzi should not go unmentioned for their acts of leadership and courage. Nor should Pte. Whewall be forgotten, who fought with his rifle and operated his wireless set at the same time and while the enemy were registering the area with shell and mortar fire. It would take too long to tell of all the deeds in detail, so let the story of L./Cpl. H. J. C. Ash suffice as being a typical Devon effort.

L./Cpl. Ash found that his section commander and several men in his section had been killed. He led the remaining two men forward under fire from machine guns and tanks. His small party was charged by eight Germans. Six of these were killed, he personally killing three of them, and the other two surrendered. He then held on to the position he had captured until he was relieved later in the day.

Documents subsequently captured showed the importance of the Regalbuto feature to the Germans. The Germans had selected three lines on which to cover their withdrawal. The first line ran from Troina through Regalbuto to Catenannova, and then along the line of the high ground to Catania. The second line ran from Troina through Regalbuto, Centuripe and Paterno to Catania. The final line ran from Troina along the line of the river to Aderno and thence to Catania. Thus it will be seen that Regalbuto was a pivot point in the two lines, and explains the stubborn resistance of the Germans in this area. A wireless intercept showed that they had been ordered to hold Regalbuto at all costs.

This action earned for us our first mention in the Canadian Divisional News-Sheet for 1st August, 1943, which contained the following account:

"FIGHT FOR REGALBUTO RIDGE

" On Friday night an English Brigade, now under command of this Division, continued their advance and secured the ridge dominating Regalbuto from the west. The Devons were detailed to hold this feature. During this morning they were counter-attacked by a battalion of Paratroops and a company of Hermann Goering Assault Engineers. After a ding-dong battle the enemy were driven off, although the Devons suffered several officer casualties. In Tunisia forty engineers of the Hermann Goering Division alone once counter-attacked a battalion position with such good effect that the battalion was routed. It is greatly to the credit of the Devons that they successfully beat off such a strong attack. *Well done, the Devons."*

The Canadians' estimate of the German forces in the Regalbuto area is somewhat optimistic. Lieut.-Colonel Valentine's estimate of two companies and several tanks is nearer the mark. Nevertheless, they were picked troops and their numbers do not detract from the Devons' victory.

CHAPTER XII

" MALTA—MARZAMEMI—MESSINA"

BY THE CAPTURE OF REGALBUTO RIDGE, the Devons had secured the dominating feature of the whole area, but this in itself was not sufficient to secure control of the town, for which the Germans were still putting up a stubborn defence. Regalbuto Ridge, however, provided a firm base on which to initiate encircling movements either on the north or south of the town. The Dorsets were now free to make another attack and at 1145 hrs. on 31st July an action commenced against a feature to the left of the road level with but below Regalbuto Ridge. The attack was supported by a strong creeping barrage provided by all the Divisional artillery.

The Brigade Group had now become such a pliable fighting weapon that the Brigadier was able to plan and launch such an attack about two hours after the situation had clarified on Regalbuto Ridge. Once again the advantage of having the Commanding Officer with the forward troops was clearly proved. Anyone who left the forefront of the battle for a few hours returned to find the position completely changed. After Regalbuto Ridge the Brigade I.O. had gone back to Brigade H.Q. for breakfast; he then returned with the intention of re-visiting the Devons and using the short cut across open country instead of the road. The Dorsets' attack had been planned in his absence, and he had no knowledge of it, with the result that he very nearly walked into the supporting barrage.

The Dorsets' attack was made by three companies. " A " Company led, with " C " and " B " Companies following. " A " Company's objective was the railway station, and this they captured without much difficulty. " C " Company then passed through and directed their attack against the higher ground above the station. Soon they came in contact with Germans who were hiding in a cemetery. A platoon sergeant was sniped and killed by the defenders, and at this the rest of the platoon went fighting mad. Some very close and bloody fighting took place with grenade and bayonet among the tombstones, and the Dorsets finally captured the position after killing 25 Germans and capturing a further 20. Apart from the sergeant, they had only one officer and one other rank wounded. In addition, they captured a large quantity of enemy weapons and ammunition.

A Canadian battalion, the 48th Highlanders, then came up in rear of the Dorsets and they were able to advance all three companies on to the high ground at the outskirts of the town. It was intended to launch an attack immediately against the town itself, but as enemy tanks had been encountered, and the Dorsets had been unable to get their anti-tank guns up on to this extremely rough feature, the attack was postponed until the following day.

Meantime, " D " Company of the Dorsets, under Capt. D. V. Wakeley, had been directed round the other side of Regalbuto Ridge with the object of capturing a steep conical hill called Tower Hill because of the building on the summit, and from which it was possible to look down on to the streets of the town. It was intended to give artillery support to this company also, but by some mischance Capt. Wakeley was not told about this and his company set off alone and unsupported. As soon as the Brigade Commander heard about this the Brigade I.O. was sent to contact " D " Company, but he could make little progress along the track, as enemy machine-gun fire compelled him and the Hampshire company which were moving into position in front of Regalbuto Ridge to take cover.

Nothing was heard of " D " Company until much later in the afternoon. A message was then received to the effect that Tower Hill was not a continuation of Regalbuto Ridge as we had suspected, but an entirely separate feature. A steep valley separated the two in which lay the houses of the outskirts of Regalbuto. Enemy tanks had appeared, and the Dorset company had fired a shot with a 6-pounder which just missed. The tanks took cover behind the houses and were pinned down. So also were the Dorset company, who were unable to proceed with the attack against Tower Hill.

Another attempt to capture Tower Hill was made by " D " Company that night, but the position was too strongly defended. This night attack was really in the nature of a fighting reconnaissance patrol to gain information to enable the 1st Canadian

Brigade, who by this time had moved round to the south of Regalbuto Ridge, to launch a brigade attack against the feature. The Dorset company, however, were too far ahead, and the report of the situation on Tower Hill was not received in time, and the Canadian attack had to be postponed. After this " D " Company were withdrawn and placed in reserve. These two skirmishing actions did credit to the leadership of Capt. Wakeley. He was right out ahead of the rest of the Brigade in country that might have been designed for ambush. Had he not had complete control over his company they might easily have been cut off and annihilated.

At first light on 1st August " A " and " B " Companies of the Dorsets, supported by artillery fire and fire from a squadron of tanks, attacked the town. They quickly accomplished their tasks and after some street fighting secured positions in the market place. It was then discovered that the approaches to the town from the west were not clear of the enemy and some enemy tanks had worked round in a position between these two companies and the remainder of the battalion. A withdrawal was therefore ordered, and this was successfully completed by midday.

During the morning General Simmonds had visited Brigade H.Q., and had outlined a future plan for the Division. Briefly, the plan consisted of a pincers movement on Regalbuto with a Canadian brigade on each flank. 231 Brigade were to remain in their present positions and provide a firm base for these operations.

The Canadians appeared to be rather slow in getting their troops into position, and on the morning of 2nd August the town of Regalbuto was still uncaptured. Accompanied by Lieut. Tucker, Brigade L.O., and Major Osmond of 165 Field Regiment, the Brigade Commander visited the Dorsets' H.Q. Lieut. Tucker was sent on ahead to find out the position. On the outskirts of the town he contacted Lieut. Lushington and after having proceeded farther he returned with the information that the town was apparently deserted. Without an escort the Brigade Commander, Major Osmond and Lieut. Tucker then proceeded on foot right through the town. The Canadians were still approaching the town and the Brigade Commander was determined that the credit of capturing Regalbuto should go to 231 Brigade, who had done most of the fighting. The party separated—the Brigade Commander to order a company of Devons to move on to the top of Tower Hill, and Lieut. Tucker to the Dorsets with orders that a company should move into

[*Crown Copyright Reserved*

REGALBUTO.
Canadian tanks enter the town in support of the Malta Brigade.

the town immediately and take with them a paint-brush and a pot of red paint. Thus when the Canadian troops moved into the town later in the day they found painted on all the prominent buildings the distinctive Cross of the Malta Brigade.

The Brigade had now been fighting continuously for three weeks, with the exception of one day resting at Vizzini. Now we were promised a rest of at least three days, but it transpired that we were never again to see hard fighting in Sicily. Our attacks on Agira and Regalbuto had broken through the right flank of the German resistance. Afterwards the Germans fought hard for the towns of Troina, Adrano and Randazzo, but this was only to cover their troops withdrawing across the Straits of Messina.

During the next two days while we rested, the remainder of the Canadian Division passed through and directed their attack on the town of Adrano. The Regalbuto—Adrano road was heavily mined and had many demolitions, and the Canadians showed great initiative in constructing an alternative road across country in the valley north of the River Salso. The only excitement during those two days was caused by the American Air Force, who bombed us with Mitchells and then strafed us with Kittyhawks; they had mistaken Regalbuto for Adrano, which lay ten miles away. The 3rd Canadian Brigade and 78th Division, who were moving up from the south, quickly captured Catenanuaovo and Centuripe, and they also threatened Adrano. To the north the American troops were fighting for possession of Troina and it was obvious that a friendly race was developing between American and British forces to see which would be the first to reach the last German stronghold at Randazzo.

The Adrano road was hopelessly congested with troops, and there was not the slightest prospect of the Brigade moving forward in that direction. It was hoped, however, that the Brigade Group would once again be able to take on an independent role and cross the hills to the north and attack the town of Bronte which lay on the road to Randazzo. To facilitate this move, the Hampshires were supplied with mules and pack saddlery, and the Brigade I.O. was dispatched to make a reconnaissance of the route. The only possible route was by using the Canadians' track north of the river and then striking north up a valley to a point where, according to the map, a track or footpath led across the tops of the hills. The Brigade I.O. did not make much progress up that valley. The Canadians were fighting Germans on the hills on either side of it, and after a short time he ran into a platoon of German infantry who were stealthily making their way along the dry river bed. He had seen enough, however, through his binoculars to report that the track which was marked so prominently on the map did not exist on the ground. After this, other methods of reaching Bronte were considered, but it soon became apparent that the Americans and the 78th Division were making such good progress that our services would not be required.

The Canadians also had been squeezed out of the battle by the 78th Division. They were withdrawn into Army reserve and on 6th July we were placed under command of the 78th Division. Thus we parted from the Canadians.

On 7th and 8th August we moved to a rest area in the valley between Regalbuto and Adrano. It was rather typical of the Malta Brigade that, while we were there and approximately five miles behind the real fighting, they should commence intensive training and take part in schemes and mock actions. On 12th August a gymkhana was staged. It was a comprehensive affair, as the following programme of events shows:

Serial No.	Event	Teams Taking Part	Remarks
1.	L.A.A. Gun Team Race	352 L.A.A. Battery, up to two guns per troop.	Driving with guns and rapid engagement of aircraft targets.
2.	Inter - Battn. Team Race	2nd Devons, 1st Hants, 1st Dorsets. One team per battalion.	Medley relay — D.R. to carrier; carrier to jeep; jeep to rifle section—advance over obstacles. 2-in. mortars into action.
3.	Alarm Stakes, Field Artillery	165 Field Regiment. 25-pdr. gun crews.	Man-handling guns—getting into action and laying on targets.
4.	Comic Event, Canoe Race	Infantry battalions — five teams each. Each team one cox and eight.	Units to provide own poles.
5.	Medical Team Race	Three casualties and 12 S.Bs. per battalion. Three ambulance cars, 200 Field Ambulance.	First aid, recovery and evacuation of wounded.
6.	3.7 - inch Howitzer Team Race	456 L.A.A. Battery, R.A. Six guns.	Stripping, reassembling and getting into action.

Serial No.	Event	Teams Taking Part	Remarks
7.	A./Tank Gun Team Race	300 A./T. Battery and infantry A./T. guns.	Portees driving, getting into action and rapid engagement of targets.
8.	Comic Relay	Up to six teams per major unit, up to two per minor unit. Each team one runner, one bicycle orderly, one mule courier.	Dress for runner—clean fatigue and Bren gun.

At 2230 hrs. on the night of 12th August a message was received from XXX Corps which stated that the Brigade Group had come under command of the 50th Division and would move to the Divisional area at Giarre on the east coast forthwith. Throughout the Sicilian campaign we had been fighting on the left flank.

This order meant that we were to make a move of about sixty miles and fight on the extreme right flank. The move took place the next day and good progress was made after an initial delay at the deviation at Adrano, where only one-way traffic was possible. We were rather surprised after making such a long journey to be ordered to make an attack against Piedimonte the same night with one battalion. The Hampshires were selected for the task. The attack was made and Piedimonte captured without meeting enemy opposition.

A situation now developed similar to that on the front which we had left. Only one road led to Messina, and along this road the Germans were retreating, pursued by the 50th Division as fast as the many demolitions would permit. There was no scope for the Malta Brigade, and again we were moved into a rest area in the Piedimonte—Fiumefreddo area.

On 17th August the American forces and troops of the 50th Division entered Messina, and all enemy resistance in Sicily ceased. The whole campaign had taken five weeks. The casualties in the Brigade Group for the Sicilian campaign amounted to 770. Most of these had been sustained by the infantry battalions and the 66 Field Company, R.E., each of which lost approximately a third of their strength.

We were now informed that we could expect a rest of at least a month, prior to taking part in operations in Italy. But on the 18th we were informed that we were to come under command of the XIII Corps. The meaning of this order soon became clear.

Once again we had been selected to make a combined operations assault as an independent formation. The place selected was Scilla, in Calabria. Those among us who were learned in the classics pointed out that most of the ancient mariners had come to a sticky end in the Straits of Messina between Scilla and Charybdis, and we wondered if we would be more fortunate.

No purpose would be served in relating once again the many difficulties of planning such an operation. This time, however, we had a precedent to work on, and perhaps because of that and the experience of Staff officers, planning was much simpler. Also the assault was to be made from shore to shore and there were no problems of moving troops and equipment from liner to landing craft whilst still at sea. The planning staff was formed and maps were produced, and the Brigade Commander decided that as far as possible the plan of attack should follow closely the Marzamemi pattern. And so the planning went on.

According to the usual custom, the Brigade concentrated on " spit and polish " and our turn-out brought words of congratulation from Generals and Brigadiers who visited the Brigade area, and shouts of " Bags of bull . . ." from troops of the Highland Division as they passed " Melita House," Brigade H.Q., with its whitewash and polished brasses. We were now in a land of plenty and lived among vines, nourished by the rich black volcano dust on the lower slopes of Mount Etna. Figs, tomatoes, blackberries, almonds and lemons were there for the picking. Vino was plentiful and formed the basis of many celebrations. Training continued as usual and battalions concentrated principally on the specialists, such as personnel for clearing minefields and firing the 3-inch mortar and anti-tank guns. An excellent bathing beach was discovered and a succession of parties went on swimming parades throughout the day. The Etna expedition should not go unmentioned. This had a modest beginning. Capts. Gilchrist, Whitehead and Baker decided that they would not leave Sicily until first climbing to its highest point. Lieut. Peebles, our Press representative, took up the idea and insisted that we should place a sign with the Malta Cross on it on the summit. Then the humorists got to work and the sign was designed similar to many which we had placed by diversions on the Sicilian roads. Eventually the sign displayed the Malta Cross and our serial number 23 and read as follows: " DANGER Bad Crater Ahead." The expedition carried the sign to the top on 21st August and the whole of the British Press seemed to take up the story, which was embroidered by the journalists almost out of recognition. Afterwards we heard that

MESSINA.

[Crown Copyright Reserved

Men of the Malta Brigade look across Messina Harbour and the Strait of Messina towards Italy, their next objective.

the report had appeared in the *Times of Malta* and that it gave particular pleasure to the Maltese people.

There was one note of tragedy. Lieut. Elliot, who had done such fine work as L.O., left Brigade H.Q. to rejoin the 2nd Devons, where he was promoted to Captain and assumed command of a company. Shortly afterwards while riding in a carrier he had the misfortune to pass over a stray mine and so lost his life.

On 2nd September the plan for the Brigade assault was changed. It was decided that a landing at Scilla would be too near the landing of the 5th Division in the Reggio area. A landing farther north was required and Gioja was the place selected. This change of plan made little difference to the planning and we settled down to wait for the attack by XIII Corps on the mainland which was scheduled to take place on 3rd September. The time of our attack would depend entirely on the progress made by XIII Corps. The Brigade commenced landing on 4th September and the assaulting fleet arrived off Cape Peloro, north of Messina in a heavy sea on the evening of the 5th.

Outside Regalbuto we had captured a bus. It shone in blue and silver, had a Diesel engine and was the pride and joy of Capt. Whitehead, the Brigade E.M.E. Originally it had a sign which read " Leonforte—Agira—Regalbuto." We quickly changed this to " Malta—Marzamemi—Messina." Although we had made a slight deviation by way of Egypt and the Red Sea, we had now reached the end of the journey.

CHAPTER XIII

" LEFT HOOK "

ON THE MORNING OF 5TH SEPTEMBER there was a heavy sea running in the Straits of Messina, and Rear-Admiral R. McGrigor informed the Brigade Commander that the landing operation at Gioja would not be possible that night unless the sea subsided. By midnight the waves had not decreased in size and the operation was postponed.

The following morning a practice landing was carried out on the beaches off which the ships were moored. Shortly after the exercise was completed the B.G.S. of XIII Corps visited Brigade

H.Q. He pointed out that the 5th Division had made such good progress in their advance northward that there was now no point in landing at Gioja and that if we were to land behind the enemy another landing place would have to be selected much farther to the north. The place selected for this landing was Porto San Venere near Pizzo in Calabria. This entailed a sea journey of about fifty miles, and the Brigade Commander was informed that he must be prepared to hold a bridgehead near Pizzo until the 5th Division could make contact from the south, and that this might take as long as three or four days.

We had taken about three months to plan, practise and train for the assault on Sicily. Now we were given notice slightly under a day and a half to make a similar assault on Italy. There was no time to wonder whether or not we were being asked to do the impossible. If the Brigade was to move at all at the appointed time many things had to be done and done quickly.

The assault on Gioja had been planned on the basis that the operation could be done from shore to shore in small assault landing craft. Pizzo was outside the range of these craft, which meant that they would have to be towed there by the larger landing craft (infantry). To make matters worse, there was a change in the number of the large landing ship (tanks) available to support the assault. Also No. 3 Commando was attached to the Brigade Group for the attack. This meant that a new landing table had to be prepared, ships had to be unloaded and reloaded and personnel had to change ships or be reshuffled within ships. This was a formidable task which would normally have taken many persons many days to complete. It was not generally realized that it was accomplished by only two officers in under twenty-four hours, but that was the achievement of Major W. Tuffill, the Brigade Major, and Major Healey, the Military Landing Officer attached to the Brigade.

The Brigade Commander was faced with the problem of whether or not to change the operational plan for the assault. The plan for the assault on Italy was based on the Sicilian plan used at Marzamemi, but there was no similarity between the two places as far as terrain was concerned. The ground rose gently away from the Marzamemi beaches, but at Pizzo it rose precipitously in places to 1,500 feet. A new plan would have added to the Brigade Major's planning difficulties, so the Brigadier determined once again to rely on the plan we had rehearsed so often and once carried out successfully in action. It was a wise decision, but the Brigade did not realize how much they owed to it until later, for had the battalions attempted to carry out a new scheme of assault as well as contend with all the other difficulties which arose in connection with the landing, the whole enterprise must surely have ended in disaster.

The Royal Navy was not in the fortunate position of having a well-tried plan to work on. For them a landing in a new place was an entirely different operation with new problems of navigation. Given time to prepare, as in the Sicilian landings, the Royal Navy had shown how they could take us to a given place at a given time with a mathematical precision despite all threats of the enemy. Persons who afterwards criticized the Navy for mismanagement of the Pizzo landing did not realize that they were never given a chance. The Navy were always aware of the problems of the Army and they never spared themselves whatever they were asked to do. They did not spare themselves on this occasion, but anyone who saw the conditions in which they were forced to do their briefing could not be anything else but sympathetic. It is not possible to brief forty officers in an hour in a small, crowded wardroom. Many of these officers could not even see the diagrams which Capt. Black, their Senior Naval Officer, was using to illustrate his talk. Those were the difficulties in the matter of briefing, which is a process common to both the Army and Navy. Problems peculiar to sailors which must also have arisen by the score can only be guessed at by the Army.

At 1830 hrs. on 7th September the Brigade Group sailed from the Straits of Messina to make the assault. There was still a considerable swell running. The Armada was in three groups. The first group consisted of landing craft (infantry) and carried Nos. 3 and 4 Commandos. The second group, also landing craft (infantry), carried the infantry battalions, supporting arms and Brigade H.Q. In the third group, landing craft (tanks) and landing ships (tanks) carried vehicles and stores. Pessimists said that this was only the first operation of many and that we were doomed to make assault landings behind the enemy lines all the way up the west coat of Italy. The Eighth Army, they said, could strike in many ways, and the blow which would always be allotted to us would be the left hook.

The assault was timed to take place at 0230 hrs. on 8th September. The voyage was without incident, and the craft arrived about five miles to seaward off Pizzo about 0200 hrs. and in sufficient time to make the assault as scheduled. This was about the only thing which went according to plan in the whole operation.

To understand the confusion which followed it is necessary to know what should have happened if the operation had been carried out as planned. The composition of the assaulting force was similar to that used at Marzamemi. All the elements of the Brigade Group were present, except that now 295 Field Company, R.E., under Major Woods, had taken the place of 66 Field Company, R.E. Our anti-tank battery had the assistance of a troop of 17-pounders (Pheasants) provided by 468 Anti-Tank Battery. The main difference was that Nos. 3 and 40 Commandos were placed under command. This was a novelty. We had never worked with commandos under command before. Numerically they were the equivalent of an additional battalion.

The commandos were ordered to lead the assault. At 0230 hrs., the time selected as zero hour, No. 3 Commando were to land on Green Beach at the same time that No. 40 Commando were landing on Amber Beach. No. 3 Commando were given the task of destroying certain known enemy posts and securing a road and railway junction. After this they were to assist the Dorsets in holding the battalion sector which lay nearest to the sea. No. 40 Commando were given the task of capturing Red Beach and the village of Porto San Venere, securing three vital road junctions and covering the main landing, which was to take place on Amber Beach. After this they were to come into Brigade reserve.

Positioning of the battalions was to be on the Marzamemi pattern—Dorsets right sector, Hampshires left sector and Devons in the centre. They were to develop the original bridgehead until they were holding a perimeter in the form of a half-circle with a radius of about one and a half miles. Each battalion had a frontage of about 2,000 yards.

The forward companies of the Hampshires and Dorsets were supposed to land on the beaches at 0300 hrs., *i.e.*, half an hour after the commando landing, and the remainder of the two battalions should have followed within half an hour. The Devons' landing was timed for 0330 hrs. For the purposes of landing, Red Beach was allotted to the Hampshires and Devons, and Amber Beach to the Dorsets. First light was expected to be about 0530 hrs.

So much for the plan. Now for the reality. The naval personnel who commanded the landing craft soon proved that the briefing had not been sufficient to give them a full understanding of the operational plan. They did not know where they were supposed to land, and timings meant nothing to them. It is one of the fundamental rules of combined operations that the Navy is in complete charge until the craft touch down on the beaches.

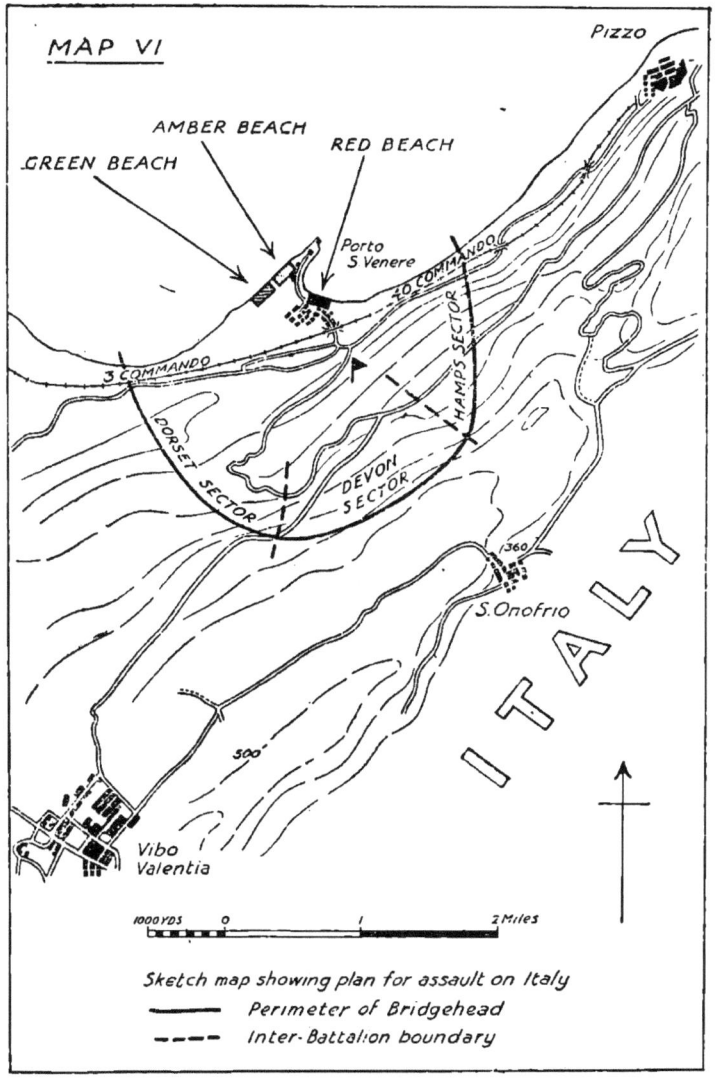

The flotillas quickly lost their formations and most of the craft were lost in the dark. Time passed and it soon became apparent that the Navy was only capable of landing in the right place by daylight. This was the worst thing which could have happened to the Army, and in most craft harsh words were exchanged between the naval commanders and the senior Army officers. The Army triumphed in the conflict of wits, but, depending on the time which the argument had taken, so did the craft land on the beaches. Thus it was that the Tactical H.Q. of the Hampshires, unsupported by any other troops, were the first to land on Italian soil. They were landed on Green Beach instead of Red Beach and were 600 yards out of position. Shortly afterwards they contacted the commandos who were landing on their right. No. 3 Commando were in more or less the right position, but No. 40 Commando were approximately 1,000 yards out. Both commandos were exactly two hours late.

At about 0500 hrs. the remainder of the Hampshire companies landed on the wrong beach (Green instead of Red), also two hours late. At the same time, the Devons were commencing to land on the wrong beach (Amber instead of Red) an hour and a half late. The Sappers should have landed with the first flights of the infantry to clear the beach of wire and mines, but they were first represented on shore by company headquarters —at 0500 hrs.—on the wrong beach. The remainder of the Sappers' company was not on the shore until an hour later. At about 0515 hrs. Brigade H.Q. and the craft carrying the Dorsets found the beaches. The Dorsets landed near to the correct beaches, but their first representative in Italy was Major R. M. Nicoll, of Battalion Rear H.Q., who was carrying a sack full of mail. The naval and beach parties who were so vital for a successful landing did not come ashore until 0530 hrs. At 0545 hrs. the first vehicles commenced off-loading from the landing craft (tanks).

A landing in the dark would have achieved complete surprise, but by now it was fully light. Troops were in full view of the enemy, who with coastal defence batteries and 88-mm. guns commenced to shell the beaches. Only one thing was in our favour—the beaches were neither mined nor wired. It was at this stage that the Brigade profited by working on a well-rehearsed plan. The commandos, who had not trained with us, did not know what to do in such an emergency, and as surprise —the element on which their shock tactics were based—had gone, their value in the landing proved to be negligible. On the other hand, at first light the battalions began to sort themselves out and move to their prearranged positions. It was the battalions with their discipline and training who thus saved the Brigade Group from what might well have been a disaster of the first magnitude.

To understand the role of the battalions it was necessary to know the topography of the area. The ground was level for about 500 yards from the beach. After that it rose sharply for about a mile up to a height of about 1,500 feet. A railway line crossed the sector in a series of cuttings and tunnels near where the ground commenced to rise. Two main roads ran right through the sector. One was a coast road and the other ran along the side of a hill at a height of about 1,000 feet. Only one lateral road connected the two main roads. This was in the Dorsets' sector and it ascended the steep hill in a series of hairpin bends. It will be seen therefore from this description that the Devons' sector, which was farthest away from the beaches and in the centre, consisted of hilltops. The Dorsets and the Hampshires who faced the flanks had part of their battalions up the hill and the other part in the low ground.

Battalion concentration areas were under shell fire. The Hampshires were the first to have a brush with the enemy. While getting into position, " B " and " C " Companies contacted enemy vehicles on the main road. Capt. D. J. Warren, who had led the advance up the difficult hill country with surprising speed, launched an immediate counter-attack.

C.S.M. Bowers and Cpl. Touzel, of the Hampshires, particularly distinguished themselves. Though under heavy fire from four German armoured fighting vehicles, they led attacks against the first vehicle with hand grenades and succeeded in knocking it out and killing all the crew. Under heavy fire they went on to put the other three vehicles out of action and wounded many of the crew. Afterwards the disabled vehicles were identified as being a 20-mm. self-propelled vierling flak multiple gun and three 3.7-inch A.A. guns, self-propelled on half-tracked chassis.

By 0730 hrs. " B " Company of the Devons, led by Major M. W. Howard, who were making their way up the steep hill, came under fire from tanks. At 0745 hrs. the 165 Field Regiment got the 3.7-inch howitzers into action near the beaches in a very exposed position.

At 0830 hrs. " A " Company of the Devons were reported to be on their objective, which was the high ground on the extreme left of the Devons' sector. At the same time, " A " Company of the Dorsets also obtained their objective after having captured 60 Italian prisoners and a coastal defence battery containing eight 155-mm. guns. Shortly after this the same company made contact with No. 3 Commando.

At about 1000 hrs. eight German Messerschmitt fighter-bombers put in an attack with machine-gun fire and small bombs against the first of the landing ships (tank) to land. The bombing was rather inaccurate and many of their bombs dropped in the village, on the beach and in assembly areas.

At 1025 hrs. " C " Company of the Devons, whose role was that of reserve company, reported that they were being attacked from the right flank. At the same time, " B " Company of the Devons, who were nearing the top of the hill, came under heavy fire from 88-mm. guns, German tanks, mortars and machine guns.

Meantime, " B " Company of the Dorsets were struggling up the hill by way of the lateral road. They were greatly encouraged by the presence of the Brigade Commander and Lieut.-Colonel Ray. Gunfire was still falling all over the area and the Brigade Commander's tam-o'-shanter bonnet was blown off his head by a near miss. The Dorsets were meeting German opposition on this road and were coming under fire of guns on half-tracked self-propelled vehicles and tanks. Sergt. E. Brown, of the Dorsets, materially assisted this advance by quickly placing his 6-pounder anti-tank gun into position and putting two of the half-tracked vehicles out of commission. He was wounded, but refused all medical assistance until he had seen the advance continue.

By midday both the Dorsets and the Hampshires were in position, and only " B " Company of the Devons had yet to take their objective. Shortly afterwards, however, they drove the German machine gunners from the top of the hill, but even then they were compelled to resist a German counter-attack supported by German mortar and 88-mm. guns. It had been a trying time for " B " Company of the Devons, and Major Howard had been compelled to fight his company throughout the morning up the steep hill against the very worst forms of German opposition.

All the battalions by now were in position, and the Devons rather faded out of the picture. Apart from the experience of " B " Company it had, by comparison, been an easy day for the " Bloody 11th."

At about 1230 hrs. a German counter-attack developed against the Dorsets on the top road. Lieut. G. Brown played a large part in withstanding this attack, which was repulsed after some very close fighting. At one time the fighting was critical.

Two of the Dorset carriers and a 6-pounder anti-tank gun had been put out of action. An armoured car seemed to be leading the spearhead of the German attack. Realizing this, Sergt. W. J. Evans, of the Dorsets, crawled along a ditch until he was near enough to throw a 36 grenade. The sergeant's aim was so accurate that he killed all the occupants of the vehicle except one officer, whom the sergeant shot whilst he was trying to make his escape.

No sooner had the Dorsets driven off the Germans than they were attacked by our own planes—again Kittyhawks. The R.A.F. were, of course, trying to shoot up the enemy, but both sides were in such close conflict that it must have been very difficult to make the distinction.

For about two hours at midday everything was quiet, and the Brigade Commander visited every unit in turn to see that the defensive positions which had been selected from the map appeared as suitable on the actual ground. He was satisfied with what he saw, but he considered that the bridgehead might be extended in the Hampshires' area, and at 1415 hrs. he ordered No. 40 Commando to patrol in the direction of Pizzo.

Shortly after the commandos had set out on this patrol, the Hampshires observed German troops assembling in a cemetery on the near side of Pizzo village. They were unable to call on the Gunners for fire to break up these concentrations of troops, as the exact location of the commandos was not known, but it was feared that they were in the same vicinity.

At this time the Hampshires were disposed as follows: " D " Company and " B " Company were forward on the left and right respectively; " C " Company were on the higher ground and disposed to meet a threat from the right flank; " A " Company were in a central position in reserve.

The Royal Navy had observing officers forward endeavouring to bring fire down on to the place where the Germans were assembling, but the fire was so badly directed that most of it fell among the commandos and " B " Company of the Hampshires. This naval fire, which came from a 15-inch monitor and flak guns firing over open sights, was devastating and caused many casualties.

Taking advantage of the confusion, the Germans launched their attack with tanks and infantry along the main road and the commandos' and Hampshires' positions came under heavy fire from 88-mm. guns and mortars. After such heavy shelling from our own and enemy guns, and with the danger of being outflanked and cut off by the German attack, the commandos were compelled to make a speedy withdrawal. " B " Company of the Hampshires were also driven back, and one platoon was lost almost to a man. The most forward platoon of " C " Company was driven down the hillside and thus linked up with the remaining platoons of " B " Company. The German tanks on the main road had been so successful that they had knocked out one 6-pounder anti-tank gun, a 15-cwt. truck and a portee. The position now was critical, for the Germans had developed the attack to both sides of the main road and the right-hand platoon of " D " Company was compelled to fall back after sustaining heavy casualties. The remaining platoons of " D " Company and the commandos were now forward on their own on the left flank, and in view of the danger of encirclement they also were withdrawn to the new line.

For the remainder of the afternoon till about 1700 hrs. dogged fighting continued, and thrust was met by counter-thrust. There were two outstanding acts of gallantry by Hampshire men. Sergt. C. Bisson found that his platoon was in danger of being surrounded at a time when they were running short of ammunition. He personally covered the withdrawal of his men so successfully by using his tommy-gun and grenades that the enemy were checked and in their turn were compelled to withdraw. Pte. M. Pook had been using his Bren gun effectively all the afternoon until he was knocked unconscious by the blast from a shell. When he regained consciousness he again attacked the enemy positions—firing the Bren gun from the hip—until he was wounded in the leg. Even then he continued to fire until he was ordered by his superior officer to seek medical assistance.

" A " Company, who were held in reserve, were then thrown into the battle and Major R. King twice led fighting patrols in an attempt to work round behind the enemy's lines. The Germans achieved a final success when they again attacked " B " Company and drove them from the feature which they commanded. This might well have proved to be a complete break through the Hampshire positions, but the 165 Field Regiment quickly brought down accurate defensive fire on to the ground which " B " Company had lost, making it impossible for the Germans to occupy it. With the approach of darkness the Germans ceased their attacks against the Hampshires and the position stabilized.

The frontage allotted to the Hampshires to cover was about 2,000 yards in length, and the distance was magnified by the uneven nature of the ground and the thick vineyards and orchards which facilitated a covered approach. Two main roads and two railway lines ran right through the middle of their sector, but there were no lateral communications and contact between the widely dispersed companies was very difficult to maintain. The observing officer for the 165 Field Regiment was in a scout car and able to move on only one of the roads where observation was not always of the best. Had this officer been in a carrier and been able to move over the rough ground, more suitable observation points could have been obtained. With all these difficulties to contend with, the Hampshires did well to hold off the enemy attack. Their determined fighting after they and the commandos had been driven back over a thousand yards undoubtedly saved the Brigade Group from a major calamity.

The danger of the whole position lay in the fact that the Brigade had no reserves except detachments of the Brigade Support Company, who used their machine guns and heavy mortars to good effect. Only half of the Support Company's mortars were able to support the Hampshires, but these succeeded in discharging 122 H.E. bombs. It was not the fault of the Brigade Commander's plan that the battalions were strung out along the perimeter in a thin red line. In view of the size of the bridgehead which is necessary to cover a maintenance beach no other dispositions are possible. There remain, therefore, the points for discussion as to whether or not in landings of this size a fourth fully equipped and trained battalion would not be more useful under command than two commandos. The point is doubly significant in the case of the Malta Brigade, whose troops can do everything which commandos can do, and more.

Darkness had now fallen and the prospect for the Brigade Group was very gloomy indeed. It had taken us all our time to hold on the first day, and yet we had been warned by Corps that we were to hold this bridgehead at all costs for three or possibly four days. The Brigade Commander ordered that all troops were to man their positions with the greatest vigilance throughout the night.

At the end of the Sicilian campaign a change had been made in the Brigade Staff officers. Capt. Cairns, of the Devons, had taken over the position of Brigade Transport Officer from Capt. Jennings. Capt. Jennings succeeded to the post of Brigade Intelligence Officer in place of Capt. Gilchrist, who had gone to XIII Corps as Liaison Officer. XIII Corps had very little news of the progress of the Pizzo fighting. A carrier pigeon, dispatched by Brigade Signals, arrived safely with the information that the landing had been successful. The wireless link was working well, but the situation changed so rapidly throughout the day that

Brigade was unable to give Corps a full situation report. The general impression back at Corps, however, was that the Brigade was meeting stiff opposition. Hearing this, Capt. Gilchrist set out about midday to contact the forward troops of the 13th Brigade, who were moving northward to join up with the Malta Brigade. The 13th Brigade were making extremely good progress, and to speed up their advance Brigadier Lorne Campbell, V.C., had formed a mobile column of all the tanks, carriers and armoured cars that he could lay his hands on. The Liaison Officer caught up with this mobile column a few miles south of Vibo Valentia just as it was going dark, and he ascertained that Brigadier Campbell had made much better progress than he had expected, but that he did not intend to move farther forward beyond the high ground south of Vibo Valentia that night. This left a gap of about six miles between the two brigades, in which lay the town itself which was thought to be unoccupied but which had not been thoroughly patrolled. Capt. Gilchrist determined to push on in front of the column and take through the news that relief was at hand. The growing darkness offered a certain amount of cover on the open road, but the town might have proved a nasty obstacle. However, instead of being met in the town by bursts of machine-gun fire, the whole of the civilian population turned out to cheer him. He did not know it at the time, but it afterwards transpired that it had been announced on the Italian wireless that Italy had surrendered unconditionally. He was the first Allied soldier to pass through the town and this was the Italian way of showing their joy at such disastrous news. At 2030 hrs. he reached Brigade Headquarters. The Germans were still shelling the beaches with flak guns and mortars, but the tension quickly relaxed when it was known that relief was at hand.

The story so far has dealt exclusively with the battles which were taking place on the perimeter. These were fierce and spasmodic, but the area of the beach was under heavy fire all day. Most of the landing craft were fired on as they came towards the beaches, but by the time landing craft (tank) and the landing ships (tank) approached the beaches the enemy gunners had the range to a nicety. The first of the landing ships (tank) was hit over and over again by all types of guns. Vehicles were set on fire, and the work in extinguishing these fires, repairing the vehicles, and removing them in order to discharge the remainder of the stores, at a time when the ship had grounded and become a sitting target, provided in itself a complete chapter of heroism. Even when these vehicle-carrying craft reached the shore the luck was still running against the Brigade, for a bulldozer, which should have been the first vehicle ashore off one of the craft, fell into the water and stuck and prevented the remainder of the cargo, consisting of guns and vehicles, from being discharged. The doors at the bows of the large landing ship (tank) jammed and this proved an unsurmountable obstacle until someone had the initiative to suggest that a bulldozer might be used to wrench them open.

For the first time all the supporting arms and services which made up the Brigade Group came into the front line with the battalions. All suffered casualties, but all stood up to the test. Brigade Headquarters sustained casualties, Capt. Cairns, the new Transport Officer, and his Transport Sergeant, both being wounded on the beach. Brigade Signals had three men killed and four men seriously wounded on board the landing ship (tank) as it sailed in. The Brigade Provost Section also had casualties, among those killed being L./Cpl. R. Pearson, who had painted the signs which had guided us through Sicily. Even such rare specialists as our photographic interpreters found themselves in the thick of the trouble. Their office truck was damaged, and while endeavouring to change a wheel Lieuts. Beresford and Puckle saw their draughtsman, Cpl. Walton, killed by a direct hit of a cannon shell.

165 Field Regiment had a very rough time and sustained many casualties. They quickly had the 3.7-inch howitzers in action and these were followed by a battery of 25-pounders. Both gun sites had of necessity to be near the beach and they were very exposed. At one time the complete teams of two guns were knocked out by enemy shell fire and this necessitated moving to another position. In this action B.S.M. Lupton was gallantly assisted by Gnr. W. E. Nixon under heavy fire. Three attempts were made to move the guns and with each attempt a gun was recovered. The fourth gun was lost only after another attempt had been made which cost the lives of three of the party and wounded three others. The Gunners also had a lively time on the roads and they lost a scout car, a quad, a 3-tonner and a 15-cwt. truck. One of these vehicles was captured intact by the enemy, and it was typical of how fortune ran that day that it should be the one that contained a complete list of secret call signs and code names. B.Q.M.S. Leigh and Bdr. A. Clemenson, of the Field Gunners, also distinguished themselves on board the landing ship (tank). It was their vehicles which were set on fire and they displayed great courage and initiative in the prompt and efficient way in which they extinguished the flames. But for

their prompt action, three lorries, each containing three tons of ammunition, would have been blown sky-high, taking the rest of the ship with them. Capt. L. Turnbull, who had so often controlled the fire of the 165 Field Regiment from dangerous positions near Agira, once again found himself under heavy machine-gun and mortar fire in the Dorsets' sector, but despite this hindrance he carried out his task so successfully that an enemy battery and two machine-gun posts were soon silenced.

352 L.A.A. Battery had one troop of six Bofors guns taking part in the landing. It had often been the complaint of Major Swatton, their cheerful commander, that his men never saw any action. Even on this day no aircraft targets presented themselves after he had got the guns on shore, but the Bofors engaged the enemy by direct fire throughout the day. The battery lost 2 men killed and 14 wounded immediately after the guns had come on shore. Gnr. E. Bingham was responsible for preventing even higher loss of life by the way in which he removed the casualties under heavy mortar fire.

The anti-tank troop of 468 Battery, who had been attached to us to supplement the guns of our own 300 Anti-Tank Battery, had the misfortune to lose one of their 17-pounder (Pheasant) guns when the Hampshires were counter-attacked. This is a new weapon and it was the first occasion on which a gun of this type had fallen into enemy hands. Fortunately in our advance the following day the gun was recaptured intact.

295 Field Company, R.E., had an unusual day. They had been landed in the wrong order at the wrong time and in the wrong place. Fortunately their immediate services were not required, as the beaches were neither mined nor wired. They followed up the battalions and carried out their other tasks of preparing road blocks and obstacles and laying anti-tank mines on the roads at the perimeter. The remainder of the company assisted in the unloading of stores near the beach and five men were wounded when a shell fell among the Company H.Q. Two men were also wounded while manning a road block when the Hampshires were counter-attacked. An unusual task performed was the blocking of a railway tunnel. This was being used by the Field Ambulance as a dressing station and until the Royal Engineers carried out their work was open to the enemy at one end. At the end of the day the Brigade Commander placed all available Sappers in Brigade reserve to act as infantry, but in this capacity they were not used.

The wonderful work done by the R.E.M.E. has not been fully appreciated. After coming under heavy gun and mortar fire, the first landing ship (tank) was badly disabled. The doors of the tank hold were jammed and the lift machinery was out of action. Vehicles on the top deck were on fire and others were disabled by the fragments of shell and bomb which had hit them. As soon as the ship beached it was dive-bombed, but this did not prevent A.S.M. Lloyd from going on board and attending to all vehicles which were in need of repair. It was principally due to his efforts and the assistance of Capt. Whitehead and A.S.M. Dew, who left Brigade H.Q. to join him, that the 165 Field Regiment were able to get a troop of 25-pounders into action so early in the battle. All three worked on the beach and on the ship under heavy fire all day and only left their exposed location after the ship had been entirely cleared of vehicles.

The main dressing station of 200 Field Ambulance arrived on the beaches about the same time as the Devons and Dorsets and established themselves in a building near by. By 0700 hrs. the field surgical unit had started to operate when the first casualties began to arrive. The landing ship (tank) touched down on the beach close to the main dressing station and this immediately attracted enemy fire. Major M. E. M. Herford and Cpl. H. F. Jessup set a fine example to the stretcher-bearers of the 200 Field Ambulance by the courageous way in which they led them in evacuating casualties from the ship under fire. Then a bomb exploded at the main dressing station and four R.A.M.C. personnel were buried in the debris but were fortunate enough to be dug out alive. After more shelling and mortar fire the main dressing station was compelled to move into a tunnel where sufficient accommodation was made for 169 casualties. The field surgical unit and field transfusion unit were also compelled to move to safer premises, but despite all these difficulties they were able to carry out thirty-three operations in as many hours.

The R.A.S.C. were represented on shore by three officers and fourteen other ranks, and five 3-ton trucks constituted the whole of their second-line transport. Nevertheless, on the first day they moved from the ship to the dump 100 tons of ammunition and 20 tons of rations. It was essential that the rations be got on shore quickly. Owing to the delay at Messina the forty-eight-hour mess-tin ration had been consumed, and units were by no means certain of getting the vehicles which contained reserves of rations. The ration strength for the landing was about 5,000 and the feeding problem was acute. The beach-brick stevedore parties were able to give little assistance nor did they realize the particular urgency of the matter, so, led by Major Belcher and Capt. Hurman, the R.A.S.C. commenced to do their own unloading. A large party of Italian prisoners were impressed to assist in the work, which was carried out under constant fire, by which four men were wounded. Eventually a dump was established about 400 yards away from the beach, but this could be seen by the enemy and drew constant fire. The only commodity liable to immediate explosion was a ton of gelignite which was placed some distance away in a separate dump. The R.A.S.C. personnel saw a mortar bomb drop right alongside the gelignite. By some miracle the gelignite did not explode, although afterwards it was found to have fallen into the crater made by the mortar bomb.

The prisoner-of-war identifications showed that we were opposed by troops of the Italian Savona Division and Germans of the 302 Mobile A.A. Regiment. There must have been other German forces involved, but the Germans are so experienced in withdrawing quickly and taking their dead and wounded with them that no other identifications were obtained. Prisoners declared that the Mobile A.A. Regiment joined battle with us by mistake. They were withdrawing before the troops of the 5th Division and they were completely surprised to find us landing behind them and barring their line of retreat. But reports from all battalion sectors speak of attacks by German infantry and tanks. How can this be explained? There are two possible theories. A self-propelled artillery regiment was known to be covering the German withdrawal from Calabria. Their old leaguer areas could be seen in several places down the main road. So also could the distinctive sign of a German self-propelled artillery regiment. It is possible, therefore, that these vehicles were mistaken for tanks. It takes an expert to distinguish between the two, because the guns are frequently mounted on tank chassis, and similar mistakes had been made in Sicily. If this theory is correct, then the so-called infantry was probably made up of those members of the artillery regiment who would normally travel in lorries. The second theory is that we were opposed by a small German battle group composed of elements of all arms. The Germans are fond of using such groups, but there is no positive evidence of its existence in this case.

The 8th September was the hardest day's fighting that the Brigade Group has ever known. It ended in triumph, but at times it came very near to disaster. The factors which turned the tide of battle were, firstly, the leadership of the Brigade Commander, who methodically set about making order out of chaos. Secondly, the battalions, who because of their training and discipline were able to move into positions with drill-like precision.

Lastly, there was the heroism of individuals, representative of all units in the Brigade Group, who refused to acknowledge the dangers of the enemy shelling or be diverted from their set purpose.

About midnight after the patrols of the 13th Brigade and the Malta Brigade had made contact, Major-General Bucknell, Commander of the 5th Division, and Brigadier Lorne Campbell, V.C., visited Brigade H.Q. The Brigade Commander was informed that the Brigade Group would come under command of the 5th Division immediately and would lead the attack northward on the following day. This was an exacting demand on a brigade which had been through such a hard day's fighting, but the only concession which the Brigade Commander asked for was that we should not have to commence the advance too early. Accordingly, at 0900 hrs. on the following day the Brigade set out to gain the line of the River Angitola with the Devons as the leading unit.

The column quickly reached the line of the river, but found that the bridge had been completely demolished by the bombing of our own planes some days earlier. The Germans themselves had been compelled to make a diversion and bridge the river in another place, but after they had crossed over they had destroyed the bridge and scattered anti-tank and anti-personnel mines all over the area. No movement forward, therefore, was possible until the 295 Field Company, R.E., had cleared the area of mines and constructed another bridge. But this took time and vehicles began to get badly congested on the road. Part of the Divisional reconnaissance unit which had been allotted to us to lead the advance were unable to get through the traffic jam.

The infantry had already crossed the river and by 1600 hrs. were marching several miles ahead unsupported by any other arms. The Brigade Commander was very anxious that the carriers should cross the river and catch up with the infantry as soon as possible, so he decided to act as his own reconnaissance unit. Before the valley and the roads had been cleared of mines he went through in his jeep. It was a tremendous risk to take, because, although he had one Sapper with him and they lifted the mines wherever they happened to see them, many other mines were lifted near by long after he had gone through.

By about 1700 hrs. the bridge was completed and the transport began to pass over. The infantry had met little opposition and the intention was to take up positions south of the River Amato for the night. At 1800 hrs. the infantry, who had already marched about sixteen miles, were still four miles short of the river and it was beginning to get dark. The leading troops were held up by machine-gun fire and, according to his usual custom, the Brigade Commander went right forward in his jeep to see what was happening. This time fortune was against him. At the far end of the stretch of road, which was dead straight for about 1,000 yards, a German armoured car was waiting. A shell from this armoured car hit the front of the jeep and burst in the back. The Brigade Commander was slightly wounded, Capt. Jennings, the Brigade I.O., received serious wounds in the foot and thigh, and the wireless operator was killed outright. Lieut.-Colonel Ray, who was seated on the bonnet of the car at the time, was extremely lucky to escape without any injuries.

Battalions were very late in getting into their positions that night, as the Germans had decided to cover their withdrawal by heavy machine-gun and mortar fire. Not much fighting had been encountered that day, but it was a creditable performance for the infantry to march twenty miles after their experiences on the previous day round the bridgehead. We did not know it at this time, but this was the last fighting which we were to see in the Italian campaign.

The Brigade moved another 200 miles northwards in the next few days. This journey was done in two stages and all personnel who could not be carried in vehicles were transported by sea. On 18th September the Brigade had reached the coastal town of Sapri; but by this time patrols of the 5th Division had contacted the Fifth Army and American forces in the Salerno area and for the time being the Eighth Army had completed its task and had now halted to reorganize.

On 20th September it was announced that all the men of Brigade H.Q. and in the battalions who had either served in Malta or fought right through the Sicilian campaign were being sent home to England. For years in Malta the boat which would some day take us home had held a prominent place in our day-dreams. Those dreams had become a reality at last, but it took several days for some of us to convince ourselves that we were really awake.

Chapter XIV

"THE OLD ORDER CHANGES"

Extract from the personal diary:

"'I am going to detail you to write up the Brigade History,' said the Brigadier. 'Right, sir!' I said, and left him to think over the implication of this change.

"I am sorry to leave Intelligence, but the idea of writing a book rather fascinates me.

"I am also a little overawed, for the story that I have to tell is the greatest story in the world at the moment.

"There will be no difficulty in 'writing up' the Malta Brigade. The difficulty will be in 'writing it down' in case those who read at some future time will say, 'This is too good to be true,' or, 'This is a prejudiced account and for propaganda.'

"So I search my mind to find some of the discreditable things we did to leaven the solid mass of successes. Above all things, I must be truthful and outspoken—and to hell with tact and diplomacy."

It had often been said about the Malta Brigade whilst it was still in Malta that the troops would be useless in modern battle. The length of time for training to fit us for real warfare was estimated at anything from six months to two years. The main charge in our indictment was that we were static and could not be relied upon to move even two miles without hopeless confusion. It was also implied, but never said openly, that we were dead on our feet and that what had once been good battalions had rotted away.

We confounded those gloomy prophets in every particular. In three and a half months not only did we train to take our part in the most specialized form of modern warfare but we changed from a brigade to a brigade group and equipped ourselves from scratch. We made two landings. The first landing went exactly to plan and it is submitted that it was the most successful combined operation which had been carried out by any part of the forces of the United Nations up to that time, and might well be studied in the future as a model and a precedent. In the second landing nearly everything went wrong. It was almost like an exercise in which difficult situations are produced to see how the exercising troops will react. This ordeal we passed through with credit.

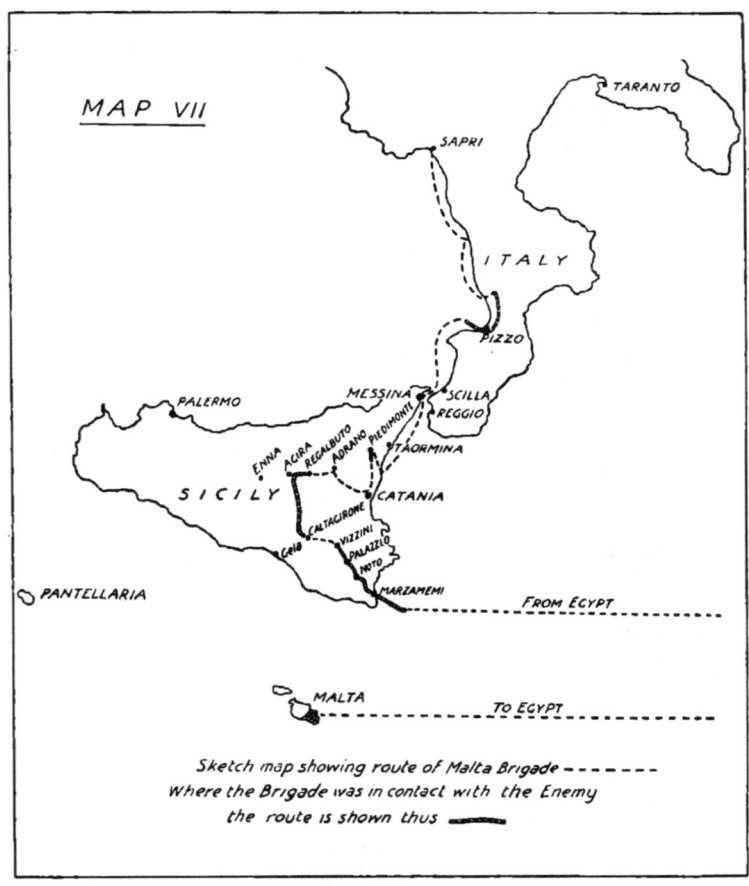

In land warfare we quickly justified our place in the Eighth Army, and it was acknowledged that there was no better fighting brigade in Sicily. We gave a perfect demonstration of how a brigade group in a mobile role, when boldly handled, could do the work of a whole division. But the greatest surprise of all was that instead of being dead on our feet we found that we could move faster and quickly outdistance everyone else. Nor did we break up our transport with this haste, because statistics proved at the end of the Sicilian campaign that we had a higher percentage of the original vehicles intact on the road than any other brigade.

Against what sort of opposition did we win our battles? Always we had superiority in numbers and equipment. As opponents, the Italian Army in Sicily could be entirely discounted, but few people realized that the Allied forces in Sicily outnumbered the Germans by at least six to one. On the other hand, we fought the cream of the German Army on battle grounds which they had selected themselves and which invariably gave great advantage to the defending troops. The Germans were certain to lose Sicily. It was only a matter of time before their line was stretched to breaking point or could stretch no more without being outflanked. But it can fairly be claimed that the Malta Brigade played a very large part in speeding up the Allied victory, for on the left flank of the Eighth Army their manœuvrability and hitting-power never gave the Germans a chance to settle. How, then, did this alleged dead-alive Brigade acquire its power?

The Brigade derived most of its strength from its Commander, Brigadier R. E. Urquhart, D.S.O. He was essentially a soldier's ideal soldier with a fine bearing and commanding presence and at all times a strict disciplinarian, but he also delighted those among us who still considered ourselves civilians—acting soldiers—and preferred business to Army methods. He had the quality—so rare in the Army—of knowing at any time exactly what had to be done, of being able to make up his mind quickly, and acting on that decision with speed and precision. His handling of a brigade group in an independent role was masterly. He could organize the most complicated attack and launch it within a few hours and he could repeat the process for days, if necessary, without tiring. In his untirable energy lay his greatest weakness, for he was liable to forget that others had not the same stamina, and on one occasion—south of Agira—he nearly drove the battalions beyond even their powers of endurance.

Most commanders, having prepared an attack, would be content to sit back and watch it run to fruition—but not so Brigadier Urquhart. He could not resist throwing himself at the enemy and then dragging the rest of the Brigade after him. He drew on the bank of fortune in a most brazen manner. He was just as liable to be killed or wounded as he stood in the open alongside a tank, on the first day of the fighting whilst a tank battle was in progress, as he was in Italy on the last day of the fighting. The impetus given to the attack by having a commander so far forward was dynamic and cannot be estimated. Nor is it possible to estimate the addition he gave to the morale of the troops when he constantly appeared among them—standing erect as if on a drill parade—while they were crouching in their slit trenches. The effect was startling.

There have been other commanders in the Eighth Army who have been renowned for similar feats—but their bravery has often been tainted by the fact that they were foolhardy or just plain stupid, and could not recognize danger or weigh the consequences of their actions. Such a thing could not be said of the Brigade Commander. He was quick to realize the danger in which others were placed, and therefore it follows that he knew exactly the risks he took himself. The history of the Brigade Group is full of acts of bravery done in the heat of battle, but this cold-blooded courage is the finest of all. That the Brigade might drive victoriously on, Brigadier Urquhart risked his life over and over again. His Staff officers made quite sure that he was awarded the D.S.O., but the decoration was really inadequate, for he had earned it many times.

Brigadier Urquhart has now left the Malta Brigade to take up an appointment as B.G.S. with XII Corps. With his previous experience it is a position in which he is certain to succeed, but until he is once again commanding troops in the field, the Army is deprived of one of its finest fighters.

Another source of power lay in the training and discipline of the three infantry battalions. There is no logical reason why an army should not function without the thing which is called discipline. It has been argued that the human race has reached a stage in its development where drill is no longer necessary for the conduct of a mass movement, and that the combination of independent and intelligent minds, each playing its own part, would produce better results. Theoretically this seems irrefutable, but up to the present this has never worked out in practice, and in the Malta Brigade is seen a perfect example of how strict discipline and the insistence on the perfect performance of tasks, which at times seemed trivial and an unnecessary drudgery, produced over a period of time a most formidable fighting force.

The Brigade Group would not have been able to move and fight like it did unless it was supported by good staff work. It was only possible for the Brigade Commander to spend so much time with the forward troops because he knew that the staff work and the co-ordination of the units forming the Group, and our relationship with Corps, were safely entrusted to the Brigade Major, Major W. E. F. Tuffill. Exactly the same thing applied to the battalions. What the Brigade Major did for the Brigade so did Capt. T. A. Holdsworth for the Devons, Capt. I. Methven, M.B.E., for the Hampshires, and Capt. N. H. Golding for the Dorsets—in the capacity of Adjutants. Then there was that very hard-working and efficient team on the administration and quartermaster side, which was represented at Brigade by Major F. G. Sadleir, Capt. H. M. Johnson and Sub-Conductor L. P. Mecklenburgh, the Brigade Ordnance Warrant Officer; and in the battalions by Capt. E. Labbett, Lieut. A. B. Stone and Lieut. (Qrmr.) A. W. Hatchard. Then there were the Brigade Signals, who when they assembled at Mena were inexperienced and in some cases not fully trained, but who under Capt. A. G. MacTavish and later under Capt. T. I. G. Grey were to maintain efficiently communications which were as involved as those of a division but without the advantages of the better divisional equipment. Lastly, there were the astonishing Brigade spirit and team work. The Brigade spirit had been fostered by Brigadier K. P. Smith, O.B.E., in Malta, and it was to be expected that in times of stress the battalions would work together as a single entity. But there was no reason why the other units which made up the Brigade Group should have acquired the same Brigade spirit so quickly. It just happened that it was so, with the result that when the Brigade swung into action it was a solid mass which moved and not unco-ordinated bits and pieces.

The old order changes. The Brigade Commander has left us and Lieut.-Colonel J. L. Spencer, D.S.O., M.C., has departed to assume command of a brigade of his own. Capt. Ian Methven, M.B.E., formerly Adjutant of the Hampshires, has now become a Brigade Major in the Fifth Army. Not much longer will Major W. E. F. Tuffill control Brigade Staff. His experience and efficient work as Brigade Major are certain to bring promotion. Major F. G. Sadleir talks about returning to his first love—the Infantry—and while the Army loses one of its best A.Qs., the Devons gain proportionately. And there are all our friends in the supporting arms and services whom we have left behind in Italy and Sicily: Capt. Jack Baker, surely the most good-natured policeman who ever existed; "Berry," king of photographs; Percy Thrupp, Italian-speaking interrogator; Lieut. Derek Peebles, our officer observer and war correspondent; and a hundred other names which immediately come to mind.

All these changes are in the natural course of things. But what about those changes dictated by the course of war? Two days' fighting in Italy cost the Brigade Group over 250 casualties in killed, wounded and missing. Our total casualties in Sicily and Italy were over 1,000, and these were incurred in twenty-three days of fighting. Many of the wounded have returned to fight again. Many of the missing will be prisoners of war in German prison camps, and some day we shall set them free. But all along that road which led so circuitously from Marzamemi to Regalbuto and near the beaches at Porto di San Venere lie the bodies of those who can only return in our memories. The old order changes. The Malta Brigade will go on, but it will never be quite the same again, for those who forged the bond and died in the faith lie buried beneath plain wooden crosses on Scraggy Top Hill, Campanelli, Regalbuto Ridge and Pizzo Beaches.

> These were no dogs of war. The earth was theirs
> And song and colour held them for their own.
> They could bestride the stars—yet not disown
> Their kinship with the lowly. They were heirs
> To all the ages. Deeds they wrought alone,
> And no one knew—so softly were they done.
>
> The simple things they loved—like children's laughter—
> Watching the patchwork scene, or on some height
> To stand alone with Nature. Theirs by right—
> Prosperity—they never knew. But after
> They were gone the paths that heroes tread
> Burned with their footprints—but Chivalry was dead.

October, 1943.

www.ingramcontent.com/pod-product-compliance
Lightning Source LLC
Chambersburg PA
CBHW071004160426
43193CB00012B/1915